SMOKE AND SOUVENIRS

THE ESSENCE OF CHARLES DEMUTH

David T. Shoemaker

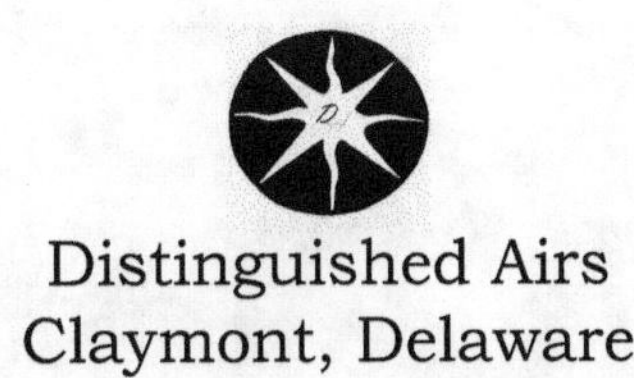

Distinguished Airs
Claymont, Delaware

PUBLISHED BY
Distinguished Airs
P.O. Box 464
Claymont, DE 19703

ISBN: 978-0-9984975-4-9
ISBN (e-book): 978-0-9984975-5-6

Interior Design: Danielle McPhail,
Sidhe na Daire Multimedia

Cover Art: David T. Shoemaker
Cover Design: Mike McPhail

All images are in the public domain and are reprinted with the support of the Demuth Foundation and the Estate of Arnold Rönnebeck.

FOR CHARLIE,

With gratitude for all
You have given me

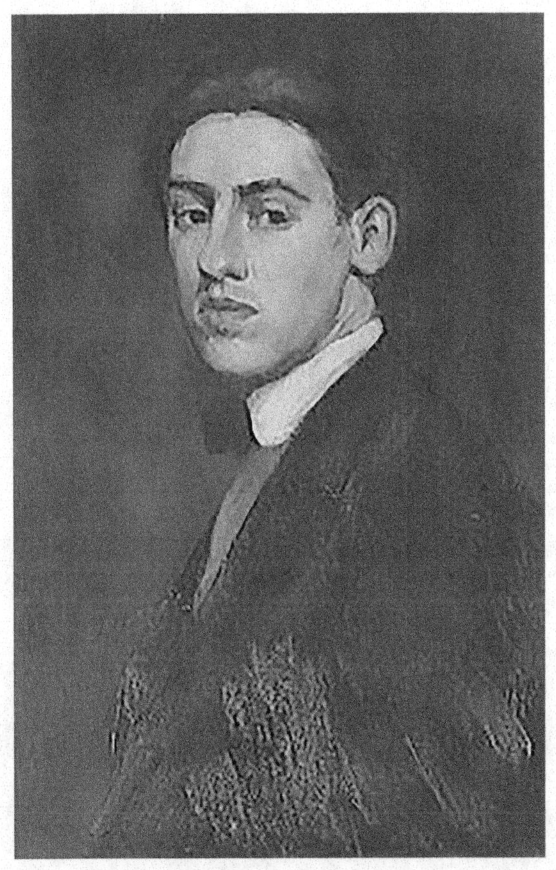

&

Abby, Emily, Greta, and Marlin
At the Demuth Foundation
For their ongoing support and encouragement.

TABLE OF CONTENTS

INTRODUCTION

When David T. Shoemaker first presented me with the material for this book, he asked me to be honest with him and expressed concern that it might feel too much like fan fiction. To my mind, it wouldn't be an indictment of its quality if it was, but the suggestion was still jarring to me. I feel like I know fan fiction when I see it, and this book is not exactly that, but there may be a lot to unpack in delineating why.

Indeed, there's a lot to unpack in anything Mr. Shoemaker writes. Most of it is steeped in the encyclopedic knowledge that flows freely from his brain and stems from his insatiable appetite for learning. Set against the backdrop of Demuth's friends and contemporaries, Shoemaker's poem, "The Party Abruptly Ended," explores the last days of a heartbroken Louis Holliday in a way that brings these legendary figures to life.

Some of it goes over my head—not because of any ivory tower esoterism, but rather because Shoemaker's work is crafted with great enthusiasm for the intimate details of the subject matter. Intimate details which I don't always have the context to absorb at first but are part of the vivid canvas he's creating, which in turn create the context.

When Mr. Shoemaker makes an appearance at readings, he is hands down the most creatively, thoughtfully dressed man in the room. Being something of a slouch myself, I've asked him if he understands that when a person writes as he does, the getting dressed part of the day doesn't require all that effort. To Mr. Shoemaker, drawing from Demuth's own philosophy, life is about making moments. Every word choice, fancy hat and pocket square becomes part of that living canvas.

So, when you couple such palpable adoration of Demuth art with a keen interest in Demuth's life AND philosophy, aren't you steering your compilation straight into fan-boy territory?

Here's where I see a difference.

With this work and his others, David T. Shoemaker wasn't inspired by his love and fascination with the artist to emulate Demuth's life and style but to become a better version of himself. Not surprisingly, as both a friend and a colleague, this is what he's done for me, stoking—as he will for you in this book—a passion for many things while allowing me to get there on my own terms.

Demuth's own friends and colleagues are a veritable who's who among early 20th Century American creative forces. Even if you had never heard of him, you probably know of Eugene O'Neil, Georgia O'Keefe, Gertrude Stein or William Carlos Williams. In "William Carlos Williams and Charles Demuth: Cross-Fertilization in the Arts", James E Breslin describes William Carlos as someone "whose closest friends were more apt to be painters than poets". There was a community there and all the camaraderie, competitive rivalry, intimacy and inspiration that goes with it. Breslin writes, many of Demuth's poster portraits were "dedicated to artists whom he knew well and/or admired."

But to look upon "I Saw the Figure 5 in Gold," which was inspired by Williams' poem, "The Great Figure," is to understand that while there is an interplay of inspiration between two artists, to suggest such a masterful piece was fan art is laughable—there's a lot of love for that poem baked into it, but it stands on its own.

If making moments has come to be part of Shoemaker's modus operandi, central to those moments is an understanding that living art doesn't happen in a vacuum. The impact of this, similar to Breslin's take on Demuth, takes us into a world that is "autonomous, self-referential, multi-directional: the world of the imagination." If that's fan fiction, we should all be writing it.

Dave Alden Hutchison
September 14, 2019

Reference: James E Breslin: Journal of Modern Literature, Vol. 6, No. 2 (Apr., 1977), pp. 248-263

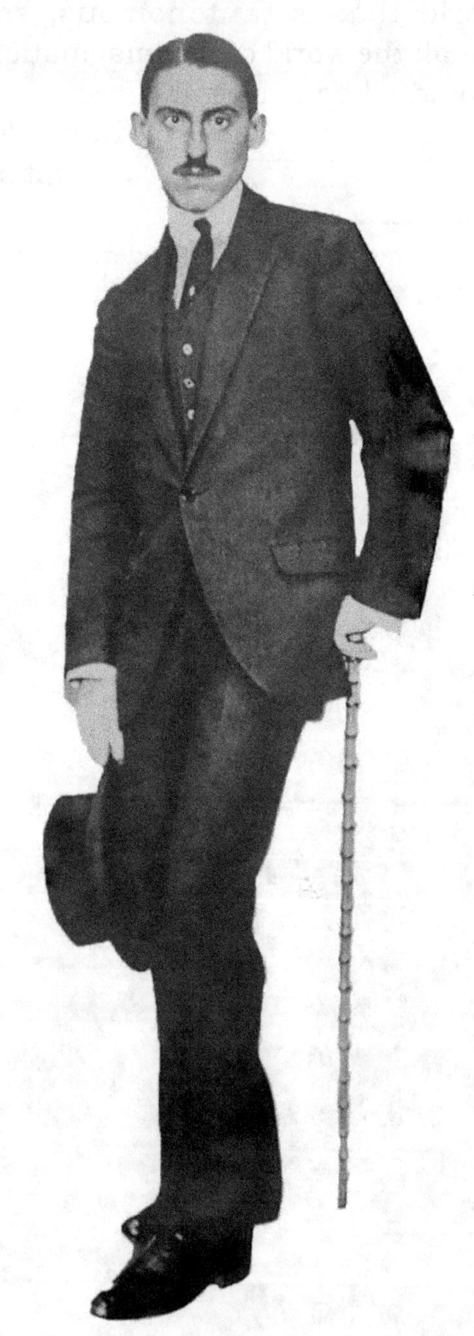

SCRIPT FOR AN INTRODUCTORY BIOGRAPHY PHOTO SHOW OF CHARLES DEMUTH FOR THE DEMUTH MUSEUM, LANCASTER PA

Welcome to the Demuth Museum, the home and studio of Charles Demuth. Or, as he jokingly referred to it: 'The Chateau'.

When he was asked to provide a brief autobiography, Demuth responded:

> *I was born November 8th, 1883, studied at the Pennsylvania Academy of the Fine Arts under William M. Chase and Thomas Anschutz.*
>
> *I went to Paris in 1907 for the first time and afterwards returned to it in 1912 and 1921, living there and in London during these visits, about 4 years in all.*
>
> *I have exhibited at the Pennsylvania Academy and the Daniel Gallery in New York City.*
>
> *I think that is the limit of my knowledge about myself. I suppose you will reply: "Know thyself, young man."[1]*

Of course, there is more to Demuth than this. He has been described as "a homosexual dandy with a whinnying laugh, a high pitched voice [with a heavy Lancaster Pennsylvania accent], black hair like patent leather…, a reddish moustache, and a sweetly malicious wit."[2]

Marsden Hartley recalled "Charles always dressed in the right degree of good taste—English taste of course—carrying his cane elegantly and for service…Because of a

---

[1] Kellner, Bruce,ed. *Letters of Charles Demuth, American Artist, 1883-1935.* Temple University Press, Philadelphia PA, 2000. P43-44

[2] Kellner: *Letters of Charles Demuth,* P. xvii-xviii

hip infirmity, he had invented a special sort of ambling walk that was so expressive of him"[3]. Susan Watts Street pointed out "He always sat crooked, sideways on the chair or sofa...with one shoulder higher than the other, and with his neck strained into a funny position because of where his shoulders were."[4]

The hip infirmity—probably Perthes—did not hold Demuth back, and he was known to dance, swim, hike, and play golf before the onset of diabetes in 1920[5]. Demuth was fortunate that his patron Dr. Albert C. Barnes referred him to Dr. Frederick Allen in Morristown, NJ, one of the leading specialists in diabetic care at the time. Under Dr. Allen's care, Demuth became one of the first patients treated with insulin in the United States. This treatment prolonged his life by a decade and allowed him to complete many of his most famous paintings—paintings that founded the Precisionist Movement, helped to define an American Style of Art, and which would inspire Abstract Expressionism and the Pop Art movement.

Demuth was very modest about his work and genuinely appreciated it when others liked it, though he would often deploy a self-deprecating wit in response. When Carl van Vechten wrote in an essay in The Reviewers: "How beautiful and terrible the flowers: Daisies with cabalistic secrets, cyclamens rosy with vice, orchids wet with the mystery of the Rosicrucians!"[6], Demuth wrote back:

---

[3] Harley, Marsden. "Farewell, Charles": *The New Caravan*. W.W.Norton & Co. Inc, New York, 1936. P.554-555

[4] Farnham, Emily, *Charles Demuth: Behind a Laughing Mask*. University of Oklahoma Press, Norton OK, 1971. P.40

[5] Haskell, Barbara. *Charles Demuth*. Whitney Museum of American Art and Harry N. Abrams, Inc. Publishers, New York, 1987. P.12-13

[6] Norton, Thomas E. *Homage to Charles Demuth*. Science Press, Ephrata PA, 1978. P.100

"Dear Carl—

I had to wait until I reached the capital, and, en route to a "rest cure", before I could write you about the "flower" article.

Your very frisky and urbane lines about me made me wish that I could be as naughty as you imagine; perhaps I can after the "Cure", dear Carl.

The article was very sympathetic, and unlike most did not rest on the words "Beauty" and "Art".

Thanks.

Yours,
Demuth"[7]

On hearing that the hallowed Metropolitan Museum had purchased one of his paintings, Demuth wrote: "Must one now I wonder feel 'old mastery'? I hope not!"[8]

Demuth was very reluctant to talk about his paintings—especially the deeper meanings or hidden truths. In an article for the journal "Creative Art", Demuth wrote:

I have been urged by Mr. Lee Simonson—who, if he would, could do it much better—I too have other pleasures—to write about my paintings.

At the start: "Why? Haven't I, in a way, painted them?"[9]... To translate these painted sentences, whatever they may be, into words—well, try it. With the best of luck, the "Sea Change" will be great. Or, granting that a translation of this kind were successful, what would you have but what was already there, and as readable?[10]

---

[7] Kellner: *Letters of Charles Demuth*, P40-41

[8] Kellner: *Letters of Charles Demuth,* P54

[9] Farnham, Emily. *Charles Demuth: His Life, Psychology, and Works.* Vol.3. University Microfilms International, Ann Arbor MI, 1959. P.936-937

[10] Farnham: *His Life, Psychology, and Works, Vol. 3,* P.936-937

Instead, Demuth urged people to just spend time looking at paintings:

> *Paintings must be looked at and looked at—they, I think, the good ones, like it. They must be understood—and that's not the right word, either—through the eyes. No writing, no talking, no singing, no dancing will explain them. They are the Final, the nth Whoopie of sight.... "Look at that!" is all that can be said before a great painting, at least by those who really see it.*[11]

So, we invite you to spend time today looking, and hope that you might experience what Demuth referred to as a "Moment": a brief, transcendent period of time where everything is perfect, and you are overwhelmed by the power of beauty.

---

[11] Farnham: *His Life, Psychology, and Works Vol. 3*, 1959. P.938

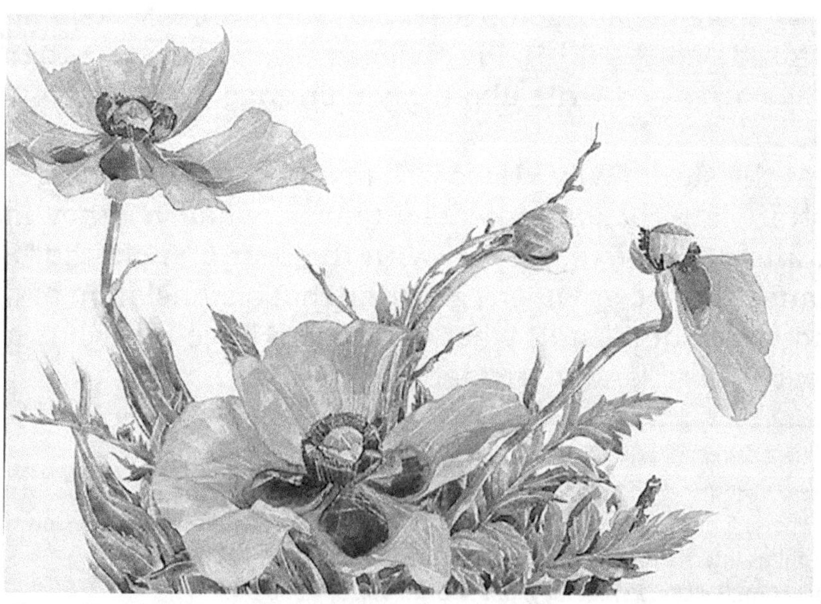

CARLOS

Two boys
On the cusp of adulthood
Sit in the dining room
Of Mrs. Chaim's boarding house.
"Would you like some prunes?"
"Yes" I replied.
That look.
It was enough.
Out went my heart to that face.
There was something soft there,
A reticence—
A welcome?—
A loneliness that called to me.
And he—
He must have seen it in me, too.
We looked,
Two young men,
And at once the bond was cemented.
Youth is so rich...
The other faces are
So many prunes!
...
After dinner
Neither wanting to return to his room
The two young men took a long walk
Together.
On Locust street
They passed a high brick wall
Above which they could see
The twisting branches of

A laurel tree.
It was very old
And neglected.
I started telling Charlie
How it must stand
In the middle of
A forgotten garden
With brick paved paths
That wind around its roots
And raised parterre beds
Now choked with weeds
Dandelions
And Forget-me-nots.
Charlie laughed
And said "Not many
Could enjoy such a thing
As that
By merely looking
At the outside of the wall!"
...
Carlos, Carlos
How good your letter did sound.
I want to answer it before I sail
And know
If I let it go much longer
It will be impossible.
I will not be able
To see you before I go—
Yes, *it is* too bad.
Still Carlos,
When I come back—
When I come back—
Well,
We may both have a start
In a small way then.

And Carlos
Even though nothing happens
After your six months work
In Boston
Don't give up.
To feel the joy of creating
For a single moment
Seems to repay one
For a year's work.
Of course, I know,
So do you,
That at times
It's hell.
When you feel like
Giving it all up
And then you think,
But what *would* become of me
If I really was made
To give it up
For ever.
Heaven be praised
Neither one of us
Will meet such a fate—
I hope.
...
"High, Higher than seventh heaven above,
Low, Lower than deepest hell beneath,
We rise and fall—you & I.
In ecstasy more full,
In sorrow more intense,
Than all these fools could ever guess,
We rise and fall—you & I.
Back and forth—
Forth to the Idea,
Back—to where?

No place or mark is there!
All this for beauty
Veiled, eternal, sure,
The essence of the morning's mist
Of feeding flocks & lovers' close embrace."
I can't remember whose this is—
Perhaps they're mine!—
One does fight at times
Especially when you expect to see
The sights of Paris within the month.
Good-bye, goodbye
With the very best wishes.

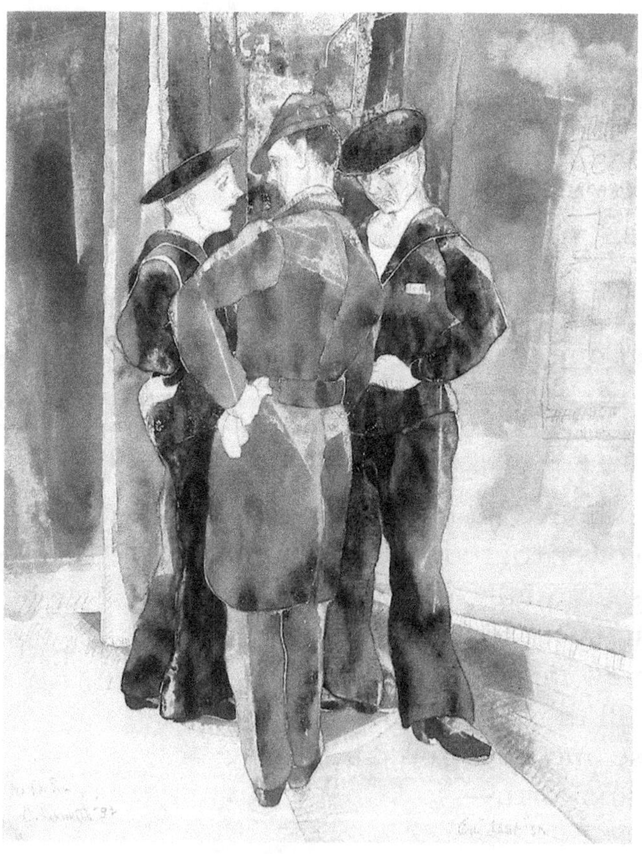

A LIVING ART

Two friends, Eddie and Charlie
Were sitting in the Golden Swan.
The morning had been given to
This and That, and the afternoon,
Again, had been wasted.
Eddie was eager to make something—
Anything—of his life.
"Let's start a magazine—
A gallery—
A theatre!"
Always a new scheme to become immortal.
In those days, the air was full of new ideas,
New styles of Art,
Of Music,
Of Dance,
Of Architecture.
It seemed every day
A new manifesto was published.
Charlie said, "Let us create a moment."
"What are you trying to say?"
"Remember yesterday, when we went
To the place that is more than a gallery—
Just a place in movement, in transition—
Well, One of the few?"
"Sure. What about it?'
"The walls were emotionally hung
With African carvings,
And there was Yellow, and Orange, and Black.
There were photographs, black and white,
Among them. A photograph of two hands."

Eddie said "Yes, So?"
Charlie replied, "Everything was perfect—
The colors, the light, the image of the hands—
It touched my soul. Time stood still.
That was a moment."
Eddie said, "Moments like that just happen.
You can't make them."
"But what if you could?
What if you dedicated your life
To bringing together the elements
Needed to make moments?
The right clothes,
The right food,
The right friends,
The right... I don't know...
Everything!
You could create a moment!"
"It would take a genius..." Eddie replied.
"But what if you lived your life to create moments,
Used each moment as a brushstroke
On the canvas of your Life.
Your Life would be a Work of Art!"
"That, my friend, would be a life worth living!"

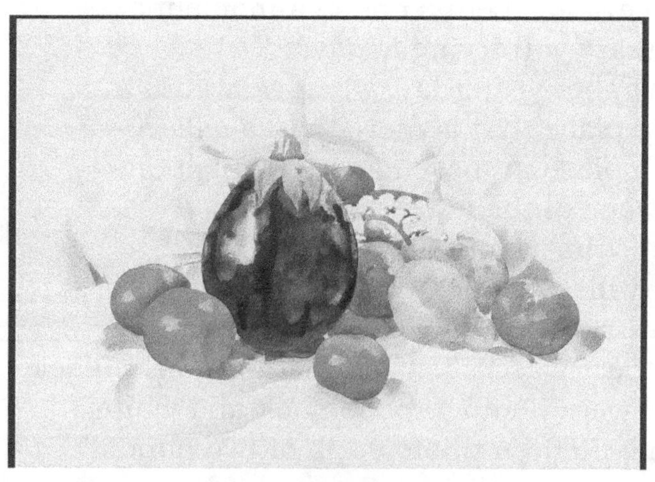

CONCERNED CITIZENS

On a cold and windy night
In Nineteen Hundred Three
Sonnichsen and Veness
Boarded Uptown train line C
They would spend the evening slumming
In the Harlem River Club
A Place to Dance,
Play Games of Chance
And Drink whiskey from a tub.
But they were on the job that night,
Not out for fun or sport.
They were there to scope the scene
Before making their report.
They were hired to be the eyes
Of the Committee of Fourteen.
Their accents mask
The secret task:
They move about unseen.

The Committee was convinced
That Modern Life's Upheaval
Was caused by Raines' Law Hotels
And the spreading Social Evil.
So they sent their lowly spies
To Eavesdrop undercover
In every Dive
And Place to Jive,
Their vices to discover.
The First thing that they noticed
As they entered the Great Hall,

Amid the crush of tables:
The Dance Floor was too small!
But this did not prevent the folks
From gaily joining in
Men danced at ease
Putting their knees
Between their partner's shins!
The dancing was indecent
With its constant Bump and Grind.
White men danced with colored girls
Instead of their own kind.
Men were dancing half undressed,
Girls wore short and skimpy knickers;
And from their mouths
Amid the howls
Came lewd, suggestive snickers.
But worse still were the men in drag,
Those bizarre, effete inverts
Who danced with other dandy fops—
The Flaming Fairy Perverts!
Yet everyone was smiling
And having a grand time.
The Pursuit of Happiness
Shouldn't be a crime!
That doesn't stop Crusaders
With their committees and their spies
From enforcing their morality
While living other lies.
That was a hundred years ago,
We think we've made progress.
But still a man can lose his job
If he prefers to wear a dress.
The Happy Warriors loudly shout
"We must safeguard every child!
No Trans people are allowed

In any room that's tiled!"
"All lives matter", they smugly say
As Black kids die in the street.
"If only they acted more like us,
Their lives would be a treat!"
"The Laws of God must override
The Laws of Man, that's plain."
Tell them that's what ISIS wants,
They'll say "It's not the same!"
It seems there's always Pharisees
To judge how others tread.
I wish they'd show compassion
And empathy instead!

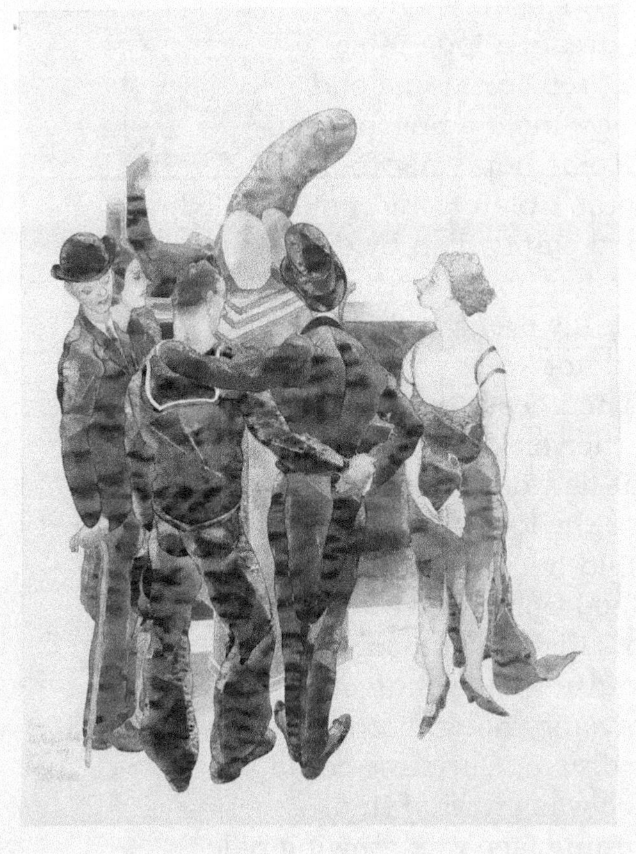

THE PARTY ABRUPTLY ENDED

(A Biography in Verse)

Prelude: Christine's Dream
    In dreams at night, he came to her
    Across the distant miles
    And though his face was clouded dark
    It always made her smile.
    But on this night, and two nights past
    His face was shining bright
    For he would soon be coming home
    To wed his heart's delight.
    In her dream a long table
    With a fireplace at one end
    Was set to hold a lavish feast
    To welcome home her friend.
    But Louie's plate could not be filled,
    It stayed empty dish by dish—
    Despite her hours at the stove
    To cook his every wish.
    She did not know what sweet to bake
    Or roasted beast to carve
    To fill the void within his soul
    So that he would not starve.
    Despite the love and care she took
    He would not eat her food—
    Only food from Louise's hand
    Would satisfy his mood.
    But Louise was feeding other men
    And gave no thought to him.
    In her dream, Christine could see
    His face was growing thin.
    His shining face was growing pale

He was quickly losing life—
Why would he choose that cruel shrew
To be his "loving" wife?
Christine awakened from this dream
With a swiftly beating heart.
Louis was due back home today
She realized with a start.
Scene 1: The Village
Before I tell this tragic tale
Of Louis' Love's displace
I must set the stage upon the page
Where these events took place.
For though such tales are often told
In every age and land
This Village had a character
The flames of passion fanned.
Among the twisted winding streets
Of Lower Manhattan Isle
A Haven grew for outcasts who
Preferred a Bohemian style.
And centered there on Washington Square
A basement café served
The Philosophical Anarchists
Who lived life unreserved.
People came from everywhere
To join this growing crowd
Filled with a restless longing
To live a life unbowed.
"When Life is very strenuous
And spirits are way down
You'd better go to Polly's
In Little Greenwich Town
For there the clans are gathered
It's there you'll find them all
The Artists and the Writers

Ranged along the wall.
Miss Polly takes the money
And Mike says he just can't
Wait any faster on the folks
In Polly's Res-tau-rant."
So with this slogan ringing loud
The hopeful masses came
To rub elbows with the Bright Young Things
Who longed for love and fame.
Among these fabled youth in town
Was Polly's younger Brother
Whose name was Louis Holliday
And Louise, who was his lover.
But Louis was not a leading light
Among the group's elite—
Tyche chose among his friends
Stars whose rise was fleet.
Chief of these was Gene O'Neill
A playwright and a drunk
Who joined the group in Provincetown
Thirty plays within his trunk.
And elegant Charlie Demuth
A young and dandy artist
Whose love Polly could not secure
Despite trying her hardest.
There's Polly's cuckhold Hippolyte
The Slavic Anarchist
Who'd yell and scream at every man
He thought Polly had kissed.
Indeed, an endless stream of words
Angrily inflected
Against Polly and all the world
Filled Hippolyte's invective!
And this despite his stated creed
That no woman should be owned;

But every time that Polly strayed
His heart began to groan.
Polly, for her part, complained
That Hippolyte had lied:
He said if Polly was not true
He would commit suicide!
But Hippolyte was widely loved
Despite his angry rants
For he's a kind and generous friend
Who loved both wine and dance.
One day he sent out 15 notes
Announcing a Trimordeur
But instead of just the 15 guests
70 came through the door!
But Hippolyte made sure there was
A table full of food
Antipasti, Spaghetti, and Red Wine
To lift everyone's mood.
The growing crowd filled up the space
There was barely room to move
So after dinner Hippolyte
Had the furniture removed.
Then a twisting, winding dance
Set to a Slavic beat
Wound its way around the room
On swiftly moving feet
There was no leader of the dance
Just a spontaneous rhythm
That led some people to spin and twirl
And others soon joined with them.
It was this freedom and joie de vie
This brotherhood of man
That drew to Greenwich Village
The outcasts of the land.
And it was in this melting pot

Of new ideas and art
That Louis met his dark Louise
And our story now can start.

Scene 2: The Journey
Louis was a lanky kid
From Evanston, Illinois
Whose mother brought him to New York
When he was just a boy.
In his teens he met Eugene
They quickly became friends
They both went off to Princeton
Though Eugene rarely attends.
The two of them lived troubled lives
Of neglect and abuse.
They tried to ease the pain of life
By drinking lots of booze.
Louis took Gene to meet his friend
A publisher of books
Who owned the Unique Book Shop
With its warm and cozy nooks.
Here a man could sit and read
About pure Anarchy
And drop off a submission
For the journal "Liberty".
In the Summer of Fourteen
Louis went to Provincetown
And there he met Charlie Demuth
The charming, witty clown.
Charlie loved to ride the bus
From Snail Road to Woods End
Urging the driver to go fast
And waving to his friends.
Among the many guests in town
Were several hopeful writers:

Susan Glaspell and Jig Cook
Would host friendly all-nighters
So next year Louis invited
Eugene to join the fray
The Provincetown Players were quickly formed
And produced Eugene's first play.
It was also here he met Christine
Though they never became lovers
They enjoyed each other's company
But pursued the love of others.
Back home they'd go to the Golden Swan
And Gene would loud recite
Poems like "The Hound of Heaven"
To the growing crowd's delight.
It was here in late sixteen
That Louis met Louise;
Her raven hair and emerald eyes
Sent quivers to his knees!
He took her to the Treasure Box
And to The Pirate's Den
And to the Ball at Webster Hall
Then home to his playpen.
Louis ran a restaurant
On MacDougal Street
Where Christine Ell cooked the food
And poets liked to meet.
Louis served them fine whisky
Along with wine and ale.
But without a liquor license
Louis was sent to jail.
From his cell Louis proposed
To "Give my heart for yours"
But Louise worried he drank too much
And said "Go work outdoors!
The sunlight and the hard labor

Will cure you of your drinking—
Return to me a sober man
And I will wear your ring!"
Louis agreed and packed his tweed
And caught the train to Utah.
The Mountain breeze and endless trees
Filled his soul with awe.
From Utah he continued west
To Oregon's fine soil
Here he found an apple farm
To pay him for his toil.
His days were spent in management
Of the apple orchard
At night he read and wrote Louise
It felt like he was tortured.
One year he did as she had asked
And never touched a drop—
Every time he thought of her
His heart would skip and hop.
But New York's a crowded place
With lots of other guys
It wasn't long before new Beaus
Appeared before her eyes.
She moved in with Edgar Varese
Who organizes sound
He said "Sound is a living thing
That must remain unbound!"
Louise and Edgar fell in love;
She started writing verse
And translating French authors
Like Rimbaud and Saint-John Perse.
She edited the Journal "Rogue"
And wrote for "The Blind Man".
Her name was mentioned with Duchamp's
Regarding his "Fountain".

But she did not tell poor Louis
While he was gone away
And so his hopes were running high
When he returned that day.
And in her dreams the sweet Christine
Who was running his café
Longed to be dear Louis' Love
If she could have her way.

Scene 3: Welcome Home
Louis' train arrived in town
On January twenty-second;
No one met him at Penn Station
"They're at work" he reckoned.
He took a cab to Polly's flat
On MacDougal Street.
He 'phoned his friends to set a time
For everyone to meet.
But Louise was not at home
Or would not take his call;
He went round and left a note
For her in the front hall.
At half past eight she finally called
With a message that was brief
She was living with another man
Louis dropped the phone in grief.
He quickly fled from Polly's flat
Straight to the Golden Swan
He stumbled into the back room
Looking dazed and growing wan.
Eugene and Agnus were both there
With Charlie and Dorothy Day
Terry Carlin and Bob Parker
Both said, "Sit here and stay!"
Despite a year of sober life

Louis began to drink
He ordered a bottle of whisky;
He did not want to think.
He'd made it through the year sober
By dreaming of Louise;
Without her there was no reason
To fight the Bum's Disease.
Some say that Louise came around
A little after midnight;
Others say she sent a note
To avoid a public fight.
Either way, Louis found out
Her heart belonged to Edgar.
She wished him well in his new life
But was lost to him forever.
This last blow was crushing hard
After all Life'd dumped on him
Quietly he made a deal
To buy some Heroin.
He kept the vial in his vest
While drinking shot on shot
And laughing 'bout the times they'd shared
Since he was just a tot.
Eugene knew there was something wrong,
A change within his friend
A darkness behind the laughing face
A wound he could not mend.
But though his heart was troubled
Gene did not say a thing
Just held Louis with his gaze
The truth from him to wring.
But Louis' mind was on the past
For he could not see a future
His heart was torn in jagged shapes
Not even God could suture.

Instead he chose to laugh with friends
About their wild times
And their stunts from the past year
Until the closing chime.

Scene 4: In the Gypsy's Caravan
Agnus went home to Waverly Place
A little before one
But the rest were not ready
To end the evening's fun.
So once the Golden Swan had closed
They went to Sheridan Square
To Romany Marie's third floor room
Up winding iron stairs.
The room was long and narrow
With a fireplace at one end
Behind which was a little room
Marie used as a kitchen.
They ordered a round of her strongest drink:
A thick Turkish Coffee.
As each finished with their cup
They showed them to Marie.
Marie would stare at the coffee grounds
Then say, stroking her chin:
"There's a shadow going out of your life
And a brightness coming in"
Or other words of encouragement
Intended to bring cheer,
But when she reached for Louis' cup
It was completely clear.
He'd drunk e'rything within the cup
No grounds were left inside
As to Louis' future fate
Marie could find no guide.
She returned the empty cup to him

With a sadly shaking head
She did not have the heart to say
That he would soon be dead.
Charlie was telling him about
The night one year before
When they snuck in the Washington Arch
Through its western door.
Up a winding brick staircase
And out onto the roof
They drank and sang and raised a flag
To give the Village proof!
But Louie's heart could not be cheered
With tales of what he'd missed;
The only thing he wished for now
Was his Louise's kiss.
No longer could he call her his—
An ache filled up his chest—
With a bitter smile he pulled
The vial from his vest.
He said, "I have some heroin,
Who will join with me?
Let's get this party off the ground
And seek our ecstasy!"
Eugene at once flew in a rage
And began to scream and shout.
If Louis was going to waste his life
He wouldn't stick about!
Gene reminded him of the times
They'd took care of one another—
He could not bear the pain of loss
Of one so like a brother.
He quickly stormed out of the room
And flew down the winding stairs
He went to Aggie at Waverly Place
To cry away his cares.

He did not tell her what was wrong
Just cried into her shoulder
But inside his heart was full of grief
As heavy as a boulder.
The others in the room were stunned
To watch Eugene depart
They had no clue what Louis had
Planned within his heart.
Louis gave the vial to Terry C,
Who inhaled a couple grains
And passed the bottle to Bob Parker
Who likewise did the same.
Charlie poured some on a spoon
And held it to his nose;
When he inhaled he felt the rush
Clear down into his toes!
He gave the vial to Louie
Who swallowed the contents whole—
He did not want to feel a rush,
Just give freedom to his soul.
Louis then slumped 'gainst Dorothy Day
Who was sitting next to him.
His eyes rolled back and face grew pale
His breaths becoming thin.
Terry and Robert quickly fled
With Louie's other friends;
Only Dorothy and Charlie stayed
With Louie to the end.
Dorothy held him in her arms
And rocked away his fears;
Charlie used his gentle hands
To wipe dear Louie's tears.
Either Bob or Terry told
Polly to go with speed
To Romany Marie's Tavern

Her Brother was in need!
But when she got there, he was gone
Still held in Dorothy's grip
But Dorothy had hid the heroin vial
In the pocket of her slip.
She told Polly he'd just collapsed
There was nothing they could do
Polly said he'd had a heart murmur
Ever since the age of two.
So, the coroner did not lie
When he wrote down "Heart Failure"
But it was not a heart attack
A doctor could have cured.
Instead, He died of a broken heart
And the loss of all his dreams.
The weight of failure and abuse
Had crushed his self esteem.

Scene 5: The Aftermath
Dorothy returned to Waverly Place
To tell Aggie and Gene
That Louis had just passed away;
The police were on the scene.
They wanted to ask a few questions
Before submitting their report.
Dorothy hid the vial from her slip
Within the davenport.
The three then left to make their way
To Romany Marie's
Along the way Eugene dropped out
For a drink his guilt to ease.
Night became day and night again
As Gene drank shot on shot
But no matter how many drinks he had
That night was not forgot.

Dorothy and Aggie continued on
And faced the inquisition:
They said Louis was just drinking,
It must be his heart condition.
Charlie wandered the streets till dawn
Blind to all around him.
His mind was locked on his friend's dear face
As his life force had grown dim.
Charlie was sensitive and must have seen
A glimpse of the other side
In Washington Square he found a bench
To collapse on and he cried.
At half past eight he staggered in
To the Hotel Breevort Café
His friend Hutch Hapgood sat there stunned
By Charlie's insane display.
Hutch said he looked like a crazy man
Like a being trapped in hell.
No sight or sound from the outside world
Could break the evil spell.
Charlie walked by without a word
And Hutch was also mute;
He'd never seen Charles in such a state
And in a wrinkled suit!
Dorothy and Aggie returned back home
To the flat at Waverly Place.
Polly arranged the undertaker
For Louis' funeral space.
On Sunday afternoon from 3 to 5
At 510 west Thirty-Fifth
His friends gathered to say farewell
And lift a glass forthwith.
With voices hushed they spoke of him
And the good times they had shared
Sad smiles and chuckles filled the room

And vows of aid declared.
Eugene arrived and quickly fled
Back to the Golden Swan
Where he stayed and drank another week
His face looked woebegone.
At last his brother Jamie drew
Eugene out of the bar
And took him back to his own flat
Inside a taxi car.
Slowly Eugene was sobered up
And knew he had to change
So he packed a bag for Provincetown
Aggie joined him on the train.
She helped him find the words to write
To describe his inner life
And agreed at last to marry him.
They were soon wed Man and Wife.
Charlie declared from that day forth
It would ever be his goal
That no man or woman would get
Their hands upon his soul.
He'd avoid the snares that Love could bring
By safeguarding his own heart
And pursue the longing of his soul
Only within his art.
He soon abandoned figure-work
To paint buildings and flowers;
Sketching faces only brought to mind
Louis' in the small hours.
Dorothy left her Press-room work
To join a nursing school;
Instead of living for herself
She'd live the Golden Rule.
She found within the Catholic Church
A path to loving Grace

She founded the Catholic Workers group
Injustice to erase.
"Food for the body is not enough;
You must also feed the soul—
Labor is a form of prayer
That can make a person whole."
And so she worked until her death
To end life's misery
And prayed Heaven would find her works
 Just and admissory.
Christine kept Louis' restaurant
And would sometimes act in plays;
In dreams at night he came to her
Until the ending of her days.

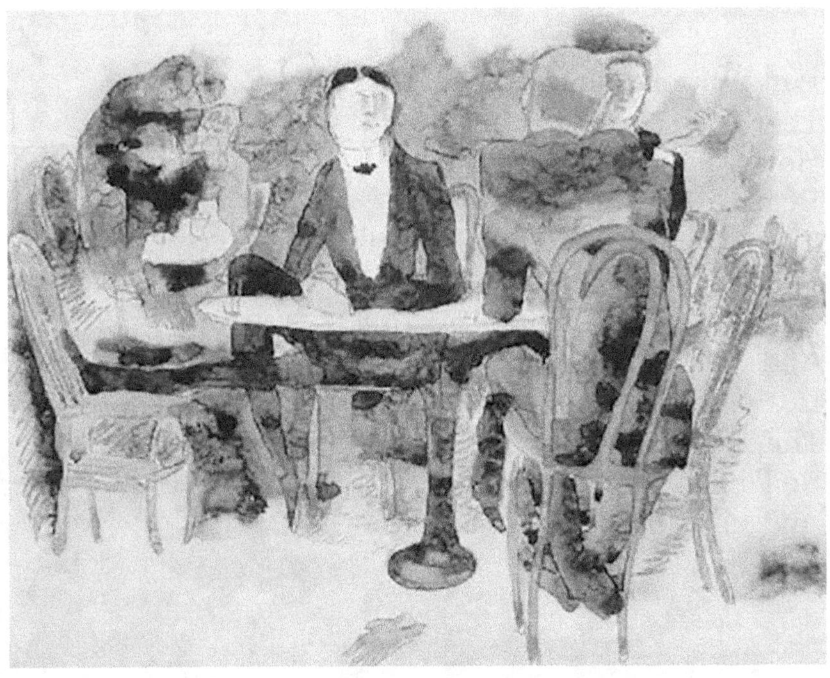

VALENTINE CONUNDRUM

The Girl:
> If of me you sometimes think,
> Return to me this Bow of Pink.
> If to me your Heart is True,
> Return to me this Bow of Blue.
> If you are another girl's Fellow,
> Return to me this Bow of Yellow.
> If to me your Heart is Dead,
> Return to me this Bow of Red.

The Boy:
> Pink, Blue, Yellow, Red;
> These are choices that I dread.
> How long am I allowed to wait
> Before I tell you of your Fate?
> There must be something I can send
> That says I like you as a Friend.
> I like the times we sit and Talk,
> And when we take an evening walk.
> But you don't make my knees go Wobbly—
> That would be your Brother Bobby!
> So I'll send you this bow of Plum
> And hope that you remain my Chum.

LITTLE DETAILS

Most people are utterly wrong.
They spend their lives
Worshiping Great Things,
Trying to experience the Infinite.
I worship the little details:
The spiraling dance
Of a yellow butterfly
Against a background of
Lush green vegetation;
The way the pink and white
Of a magnolia blossom
Pops against the deep verdant
Of its leaves;
The silky feel
Of an Eggplant's skin
As I smooth it with my finger;
The clear, amber glow—
Amber with a touch of red—
Created by a beam of sunlight
Passing through a spoonful
Of Orange Marmalade.
They say the Devil is in the Details,
But it is in the details
That I see the fingerprints of God!

CLASSIFIED PERSONAL

Stylish, Whimsical, Lonesome male
seeks ___________(?)
for companionship and completeness.
I like horses,
Charlie Chaplin movies,
Marlene Dietrich films,
Wine,
Marcel Duchamp,
Swans,
Marcel Proust,
Prize-fights,
Orchestral Music
(But definitely NOT Opera),
Ballet,
Stravinsky,
Ravel,
Ragtime,
And Robert Locher.
I prefer Plush and Wood
To Metal and Leather,
Superior trifles
To Plain living.
I abhor the commonplace.
I do not care for domestic pets
Nor for small children,
Nor people who talk about art.
I do not understand women
Nor classical music.
I know flowers.
If you like frivolities that are

Elegant in tone,
A little precious in import,
And swift in their results;
Being swept up into atmospheres;
And tiger-like stalking after amusement
 Down the courses of the night
Extend a slender white hand
From between the funnels
And I will join you in the shadows.

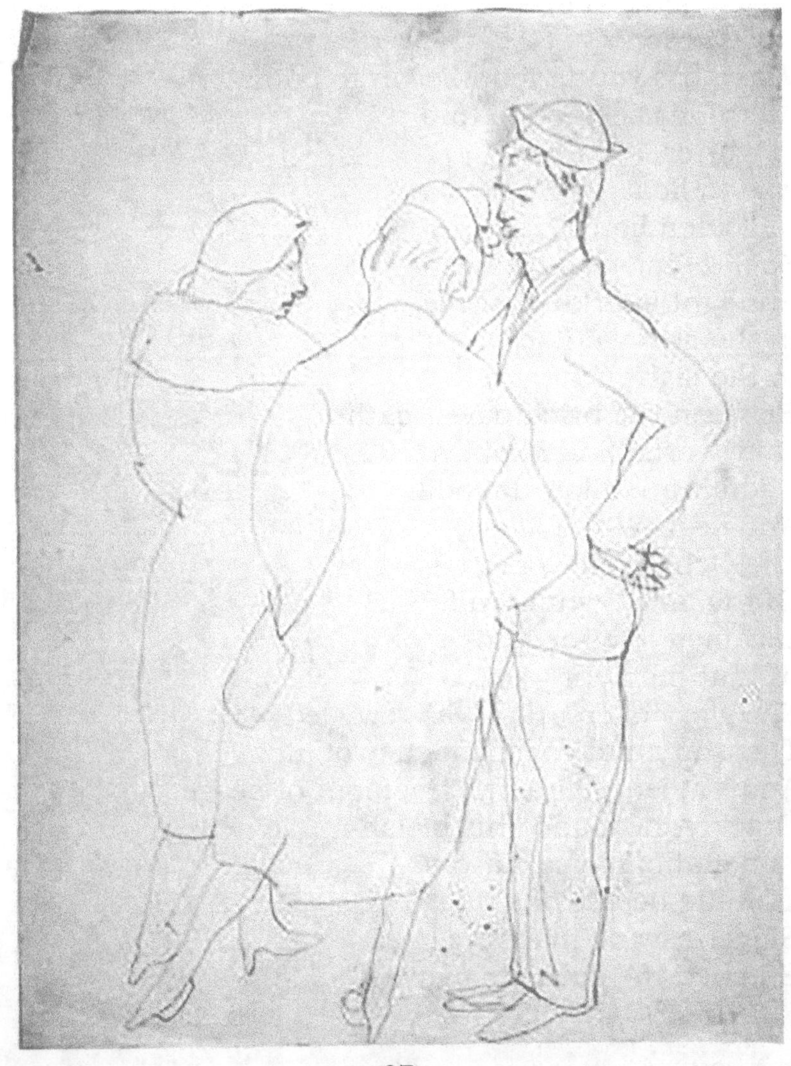

IN HOSPITAL

A man young in years
But old in his soul
And closer to his end
Than he should have been
Sat behind an easel
In a garden.
When the young man began to paint
All things seemed to him
To glitter
And to float
In golden liquid,
So dazzling was the scene.
Sunlight sparkled off the water
In the Koi pond.
In the eight triangles
Between the brick paved paths
Grew vermillion poppies
Cadmium-Yellow daffodils
And Lead-White lilies.
The Ochre yellow arches
Of the limed white walls
Gleamed like the sun.
In that moment
The glory of creation was revealed
The unity and codependency of life
And Vincent felt a brief moment of peace.
Quickly, he loaded his brush
And stabbing the canvas
Like the needle of a
Singer sewing machine
Stitched the scene to canvas.

AGAINST GREAT ODDS: THE HEALTH OF CHARLES DEMUTH

It has become part of the Demuth canon and legend that he became an artist because he was a frail and sickly child; that his poor health determined his career choice. "Because of his delicate constitution, it was no doubt decided for him that he should be developed into an artist, instead of trying to start him on a more robust sort of career" was how Laetitia Herr Malone expressed it in her tribute paper to Charles Demuth for the Lancaster County Historical Society in 1948.[1] In some ways, this is an understandable narrative: we love to celebrate individuals who overcome great odds to become successful. It gives us hope for our own futures.

But was Demuth really that frail and sickly as a child? He wrote in an unpublished short story: "The painter heard and was sorry for the child; he, too, never painted in the garden when he was its age. His paints had always been reserved for rainy days or for the times when he had been ill and he remembered that *even on these rare occasions* [author's emphasis] he only filled in outlines of animals with paint..."[2]

Alvord L. Eiseman wrote "The first four years of Charles' life can be termed uneventful, probably with the customary

[1] Malone, Mrs. John E. "Charles Demuth": *Papers Read before the Lancaster County Historical Society*. Lancaster, PA: Volume LII, No. 1, 1948. P.4

[2] Haskell, Barbara. *Charles Demuth*. New York: Whitney Museum of American Art in association with Harry N. Abrams, Inc. Publishers, 1987. P.45

childhood illnesses...later stories of his being tubercular and rickety are at best after the fact and apocryphal.[3]

The question is whether his childhood health impacted or impaired Demuth's life to the point that a career as an artist would be preferable to other professions, and by extension if Demuth was an artist by necessity instead of by choice. If he was an artist by necessity, he certainly made the most of it. It also raises the question of whether artists can be made, or if they possess some unique quality to see the world differently and talent for expressing this world-view.

There is no denying that Charles suffered from two chronic illness during his lifetime: the hip infirmity he developed around age 4 and the diabetes which was diagnosed when he was around age 37. A third, depression, was not diagnosed or treated during his lifetime but is indicated in his letters and the remembrances of his friends. The depression may be the result of living under the cloud of a terminal illness (diabetes). George Biddle wrote: "He was moody; alternating fits of deep depression and sunny gaiety. He was naturally gay and loveable, but suffered from ill health."[4]

Let's begin by looking at the hip infirmity, its treatment and effects on Charles. There are various accounts of the cause and nature of the hip infirmity, including a story reported by Emily Farnham and Alvord Eiseman that the injury resulted when his father Ferdinand was playing with Charles. They reported that Ferdinand was tossing Charles in the air one day, either in the tobacco shop or on the stoop, and missed catching him, which resulted in a broken leg. But Barbara Haskell wrote:

---

[3] Eisemann, Alvord L. *A Study in the Development of an Artist: Charles Demuth*. Ann Arbor, MI: Xerox University Microfilms, Inc. 1976. P.9

[4] Farnham, Emily. *Charles Demuth: His Life, Psychology, and Works. Vol.3*. Ann Arbor, MI: University Microfilms International. P.952

"What now seems clear from extant descriptions of Demuth's symptoms and convalescence is that he had contracted Perthes, a disease of the hip that predominately strikes boys between the ages of four and five. It leaves the child with one short leg and subject to occasional pain due to the deformation of the hip joint...Perthes was not identified until 1915, when x-rays became available for diagnostic purposes...

[M]ore important for the formation of Demuth's personality was the fact that, in his time, the prescribed "cure" for the then mysterious disease was six weeks in traction followed by one to two years in bed. During this protracted period of incapacitation, the young Demuth was totally dependent on his mother, Augusta, for even simple acts such as bathing and relieving himself. [5]

Because of the protracted period of bedrest, Charles received his earliest education at home. Here he was tutored by his Aunt Kate Buckius, his mother's sister and a teacher at the nearby South Duke Street elementary. He learned to read and was given books to pass the time, as well as drawing books and paints. Alvord L. Eiseman stated: "It is probable that the most lasting repercussion resulting from the injury, and from the enforced over a year's stay in bed and in traction, was the development of Charles' first interest in Art."[6]

Demuth certainly was given coloring books during his one to two years of bedrest during his last years at his family's 109 N. Lime Street home, but it was also during this time that he became a voracious reader. Demuth presented himself to Gertrude Stein in 1912 as an aspiring writer and listed himself as both a writer and painter

---

[5] Haskell: *Charles Demuth*, P.12-13

[6] Eisemann: *A Study in the Development of an Artist,* 1976. P.16

in the magazine *Camera Work* in 1914,[7] so it was by no means determined that he should be an artist because of the hip infirmity. In fact, every indication is that up to the age of 18, it was believed that Charles would follow in his ancestor's footsteps and become a tobacconist at the family shop.

Demuth's course of study at Franklin and Marshall was the "scientific track," geared towards mathematics and other subjects suited for the business world, which indicates that his father still held out hope that he would join the family business...

After graduating in June 1901 from Franklin and Marshall, Demuth did not, as has hitherto been believed, enroll immediately in art school but remained at home in Lancaster for more than two years."[8]

Photographs of the tobacco shop interior taken by Ferdinand show it to be full of art—in the form of Art Nouveau posters and cigar boxes and the walls of his family home were decorated with watercolor paintings and needlepoint by his great aunts. With or without a hip infirmity, Demuth would have been exposed to art.

Regarding the effects of the hip infirmity, Barbara Haskell went further: "The illness had a permanent effect far in excess of the lameness with which, apparently, he coped quite well as an adult...He was robbed of autonomy and independence at a crucial moment in his psychological development, that is, during the years of a boy's heightened social activity. It left him with a life-long self-image as an invalid, someone different from other people. He became an introvert, absorbed in a private world."[9] I find

---

[7] Haskell: *Charles Demuth,* P.35

[8] Haskell: *Charles Demuth,* P.14-15

nothing in Demuth's writings or letters to indicate he considered himself an invalid, nor that the hip infirmity was the reason he may have felt different from other people. Demuth wrote on his 1921 passport application that he was "slightly lame" under distinguishing marks.[10]

Haskell writes "even his need for a cane he transformed into a virtue by perfecting a distinctive sort of ambling gait which found appeal."[11] In this way, he has more in common with Charlie Chaplin's "The Tramp" than with an invalid. Chaplin described his character this way: "He actually became a man with a soul—a point of view. I defined to Mr. Sennett the type of person he was. He wears an air of romantic hunger, forever seeking romance, but his feet won't let him."[12]

Others have described the Tramp as a man "who endeavors to behave with the manners and dignity of a gentleman despite his actual social status."[13] The same might be said of Demuth, who cultivated an elegant and aristocratic bearing.

Lettie Malone wrote: "As the writer remembers him, he was never very strong. He will be remembered by those who knew him as somewhat lame and wore a built-up shoe. Nevertheless, he could do many things in spite of this affliction, including dancing."[14]

---

[9] Haskell: *Charles Demuth*, P.13

[10] Photocopy of original document, Collection of David T. Shoemaker

[11] Haskell: *Charles Demuth*, P.13

[12] Charlie Chaplin (November 1933), "A Comedian Sees the World", Woman's Home Companion

[13] https://en.wikipedia.org/wiki/The_Tramp

William Carlos Williams adds "In spite of his hip, he used to do a lot of walking; though he was not athletic."[15]

Based on these descriptions, there is no reason to believe that Demuth would have been physically incapable of performing any professional career. Frederick W. Hammond, a longtime friend of Charles and Augusta, said "If Charles had not been an artist, he would have been a fine architect."[16]

During the two years between graduating from the Franklin and Marshall Academy and enrolling at the Drexel Institute, Demuth worked as a clerk in the tobacco shop. It has been thought this was because Ferdinand insisted on it or was reluctant to support Charles' desire to be a professional artist. Haskell continues:

"[I]f Demuth was to be an artist, the only practical choice was to join the growing ranks of professionals doing commercial art. The applied arts fit into an applied work ethic and reflected as well the kind of art with which Demuth had been successful as a child: illustration and china painting.

In October 1903, Demuth enrolled in the Drexel Institute of Art, Science, and Industry. Located in Philadelphia, Drexel's stated aim was to train students in a variety of practical skills. It has become nationally prominent in 1894, when it opened the first department of illustration in the country.

Demuth entered Drexel as an elementary Art student, an indication of the limited nature of his Lancaster art lessons. During the summer of 1904, he stayed in Philadelphia to attend the summer session at the Pennsylvania School of Industrial

---

[14] Malone: "Charles Demuth", P.4

[15] Farnham: *His Life, Psychology, and Works. Vol.3,* P.989

[16] Malone: "Charles Demuth", P.4

Art. Although the school offered drawing courses, its curriculum was distinctly oriented toward applied arts and trades.

By the end of the [Spring 1905] term, Demuth had won two awards at Drexel: a second prize in antique drawing and an honorable mention in illustration-composition. In June, 1905, however, Drexel announced the termination of all courses in fine and applied arts in order to consolidate its resources in other departments. Demuth then transferred to the Pennsylvania Academy, where he remained through January 1910."[17]

It is interesting to note that in the Lancaster City Directories from 1901 through 1910 Charles' occupation is listed as "Clerk". It was not until after his father's death in January 1911, that it was changed to "Artist".[18]

If his lameness affected his decision to be an artist at all, it was more likely in choice of medium rather than the choice of profession. When Susan Watts Street was asked whether, in her opinion, Demuth's lameness influenced his life a great deal, she replied: "Once Demuth said to me: 'I'd much rather do watercolors. Oil paints are so messy.' For one thing, he couldn't very easily carry a heavy easel and the rest of an artist's paraphernalia to the beach. Yet Demuth took long walks and was not much hampered by his lameness."[19] Most artists—with the exception of the Impressionists—wouldn't take their easels to the beach. They would take their sketchbooks and watercolors to make preliminary

---

[17] Haskell: *Charles Demuth*, P.16-17

[18] *Lancaster City Directory*, Philadelphia: R. L. Polk and Co., 1901, 1905-06, 1907. 1909-1910; 1911-1912

sketches, then complete the finished paintings in their studios.

Demuth is known to have done this, creating many sketches on paper before beginning a major work in oil or tempera. Demuth also realized that works on paper are seldom shown and largely ignored by major museums. This may have encouraged him to begin works in Tempera and Oils starting around 1919, the same time he began experiencing symptoms of diabetes. In a review of Demuth's 1920 show at the Daniel Gallery, Henry McBride wrote: "He grows more earnest and eloquent with the times;... but he also grows more ascetic. His studies of New England and Pennsylvania would be quite terrible—if they were not so beautiful. Whether he has studied Nietzsche or not I do not know, but certainly he sees plenty of applied Nietzscheanism in this beloved but hard country of ours. Mr. Demuth must have gone through a period of terror..."[20]

During the summer of 1920, while visiting Cape Cod, Demuth "suffered the most severe diabetic attacks he had yet experienced, becoming completely incapacitated. From this time forward, Demuth lived in the shadow of death."[21]

The standard treatment for Diabetes at this time, before the discovery of insulin, was a starvation treatment. The patient would be given 500 calories a day until the urine was free of sugar, then the food intake was slowly increased to about 1200 calories. Food had to be carefully weighed, and starchy vegetables avoided.

"Starvation treatment did work in a limited sense and was welcomed by some doctors simply because they had nothing else to offer... Character was a crucial factor

---

[19] Farnham: *His Life, Psychology, and Works. Vol.3*, P.976

[20] Farnham: *Behind a Laughing Mask*, P.124

[21] Farnham: *Behind a Laughing Mask*, P.123

in the success or otherwise of under-nutrition treatment. In 1921, John R. Williams of New York claimed that most failures were due to 'unfaithfulness on the part of the patient' and nearly half of the deaths in his seventy three patients were because the treatment had been abandoned."[22]

The life expectancy for those who failed to rigorously follow the diet was thirty months before the discovery of insulin.

Demuth wrote: "Well, here I am finally put away, by my own hand. It seems very thorough!—well, rather,—but what, no doubt, I need. Very tiring,—although a wonderful place as to surrounding country... In time, I will get everything,—that seems the idea,—even sugar. Of course, so far I've been starved, that is egg and meat in very little quantities... I am bored stiff."[23]

His friend Dr. William Carlos Williams wrote: "The result was frightening. Charley faded to mere bones, but he was able to live. They occasionally permitted him to be taken home to us for a short visit but I had to return him the same evening. He brought with him a pair of scales and weighed his food carefully. I never saw a thinner person who could stand on his feet and move about."[24]

By July, 1922, Demuth wrote: "Am enclosing, I think, a very good report of myself (and garden)...hope you like it. Sorry I couldn't do something for "M.S.S." about camera. Couldn't. Very little left after I do my daily (sometimes, now weekly) painting."[25] Charles was forced to face the fact that he was nearing the end of his life. "Today my food goes up,—

---

[22] Tattersall, Robert. *Diabetes: The Biography*. Oxford: Oxford University Press, 2009. P49-50

[23] Fahlman, Betsy. *Chimneys and Towers*. University of Pennsylvania Press: Philadelphia. 2007. P.80

[24] Farnham: *Behind a Laughing Mask*. P.138

then we will see,—will let you know. I think that I'll be here, of course, for some weeks,—However, I'll go through with it now,— What else is there to do,—and I do think Allen is the real thing,—very unemotional and cold,—drives me almost mad at times,—best in the long run, I tell myself, in my sane moments."[26]

Demuth abandoned figure work in 1919 and began a period of experimentation as he tried to create a unique style which would secure his place in art history. "Between 1920 and 1922 Demuth introduced into his architectural depictions a planar format created by flattening space, broadening his forms, and extending his composition to the perimeters of the canvas. He no longer "floated" motifs or prismatically handled ambient space. Instead, he elevated shape over line as the primary compositional device. And with his substitution of oil for watercolor, the once soft radiance of his paper-thin ray lines gave way to a more opaque and uniform surface. By overlapping geometric planes to collapse depth and describe motifs, Demuth established the style that would later be known as Prescisionism."[27]

Fortunately, insulin was discovered in 1921 in Canada. It was in Morristown on August 10, 1922, that Dr. Allen first administered insulin in the United States. Demuth was reluctant to try the new treatment, but Dr. Barnes persuaded him to try it. Dr. Emily Farnham reported that Demuth was the second patient in the U.S. to receive insulin.[28]

---

[25] Fahlman: *Chimneys and Towers*. P.81

[26] Fahlman: *Chimneys and Towers*. P.80-81

[27] Haskell: *Charles Demuth*, P.130-131

[28] Farnham: *Behind a Laughing Mask*. P.138

By September, 1923, Demuth was able to write "On the other hand, I grow fat,—and fatter,—which is something! And I garden and cut grass and stay on the move,—as is expected, it seems."[29]

His mother Augusta resumed her role as Charles caretaker, carefully weighing his food and ensuring he followed his diet. Charles' strength waxed and waned depending on the strength of the insulin batch, but he quickly tired. For this reason, he focused on watercolors, particularly the still-lifes of vegetables and flowers. He would meet his mother at the kitchen door, grab the market basket from her hands, and carry it up to his studio to paint them before she could start cooking. He would sometimes ask for Eggplants with a rich color and nice form. But he never lost sight of his legacy, and he continued to produce works in oil as his strength allowed.

In November 1923, Demuth began work on his 'homages', a "series of 'posters'—emblematic portraits of American artists who were his friends and contemporaries. ...[I]n these portraits Demuth did not intend to render physical likeness, but rather to convey something of the subject's psychological and artistic character by means of commonplace objects."[30]

Demuth not only chose to honor his friends who had supported and encouraged him, but "intended his object-portraits to encompass the major personalities of American painting and writing. In this sense, the undertaking restated his conviction that the future of art rested in American hands; that modernism had been transplanted from Europe and was being transformed by the American experience."[31]

---

[29] Kellner: *Letters.* P5

[30] Haskell: *Charles Demuth*, P.173

[31] Haskell: *Charles Demuth*, P.174

Demuth worked on this series for 5 years, culminating with *The Figure 5 in Gold* and *Longhi on Broadway* in 1928.

Demuth included *The Figure 5 in Gold* in his 1929 exhibition at The Intimate Gallery, despite considering it "unfinished" at the time. His friend William Carlos Williams, the subject of the painting, considered it 'the best American picture of its time.' Barbara Haskell wrote: "It did brilliantly distill Demuth's life-long efforts to generate equivalencies between literary and visual art. Through the use of symbols, fragmented forms, and the Futurist vocabulary of his earlier Architectural work, Demuth successfully captured the multiplicity of experience inherent in a single moment."[32]

Despite this, most of the poster portraits were critically disliked. One befuddled critic declared the Demuth homages to new voices in the American grain were "in a code for which we have not the key."[33] When Demuth shipped the Marin poster to Alfred Stieglitz, he wrote that if Stieglitz liked it, "you and I will be the only two living things that do!"[34]

Discouraged, Demuth wrote to Stieglitz in July of 1926: "I've never felt so 'low'…There seems to be nothing, nothing. I haven't painted for weeks. Everything seems to have been painted…My lack of, whatever it is, which has been going on for some months, has made me think seriously of a trip abroad. A very unwise idea for me,—still."[35] This last letter is one of the clearest indications of Demuth's struggles with depression.

---

[32] Haskell: *Charles Demuth*, P.185

[33] McNally, Owen. "The Riddle Revealed": *Hartford Courant*. Hartford, CT, September 18, 1994.

[34] Haskell: *Charles Demuth*, P.182

[35] Haskell: *Charles Demuth*, P.182

In 1927, Demuth began his last great painting series: architectural paintings of Lancaster. "Lancaster remained the subject of Demuth's last group of paintings. His goal, however, was not to create a likeness of the city but to use likeness as a means through which to record his times and his response to them. It was this kind of representation that he identified as fundamental to all successful portraits."[36] In these portraits of his hometown, Demuth was struggling to create something that was both uniquely American and decidedly modern. Demuth wrote in November of 1921: "I am so tired,—maybe it is my health, but, I suspect it is more from hearing so often,—'I must go to Berlin, or Rome, or, Vienna, or, Florence, or, the East, or, the South Seas,—I know there must be something there for *me*.' I so often wished at hearing them,—that some would, or, all would go to hell. What work I do will be done here; terrible as it is to work in this 'our land of the free.'"[37] One might get the mistaken impression that Demuth didn't like America. He loved the country and the ideals upon which it was founded, but felt that the promise of those ideals did not always bear fruit, especially for artists. In an unpublished play, he wrote: "The painting is in the Boston Museum,—it is a self portrait by Washington Allston. No,—you've never heard of him,—so many American painters have never been heard of, well, he's not a discovery of mine. Henry James wrote about him. James used him as proof that America is no land for the artist. Allston went mad after returning to America from years spent in Europe. Perhaps James was right,—I know America is only for the strong. Hemingway,—yes, he lives in Europe."[38]

---

[36] Haskell: *Charles Demuth*, P.193

[37] Farnham: *His Life, Psychology, and Works. Vol.3.* P.944

[38] Farnham: *His Life, Psychology, and Works. Vol.3.* P.930

These two goals were on Demuth's mind when he thought about his legacy. He wrote to Stieglitz: "Europe was to us all nearer & dearer,—but,—well you know. What could any of us add to Europe? Perhaps, I like to suffer; at times, I think that I do. It may never flower,—this our state, but, if it does I should like to feel from some star, or whatever, that my living added a bit;—for in this flower, if it does, I can imagine Rome in its glory looking very mild."[39]

Demuth wrote to his friend William Carlos Williams in 1907: "To experience the joy of creation for just a moment seems to repay one for a year's work."[40] It was this joy he felt as an artist, more than his health issues, that persuaded Demuth to pursue a career in art. Darrell Larsen told Emily Farnham: "He said: 'I get more out of my watercolors than anybody else does."[41] Demuth wrote to Stieglitz: "so few, understand love and work; I think if a few do we may not have lived entirely without point"[42] Demuth loved to paint and undoubtedly would have painted in his free time if he had not chosen to be an artist.

And that is the important thing: He chose to be an artist. Chose to dedicate his life to creating pictures that captured the unique beauty and wonder of the American experience. "I never knew Europe was so wonderful,—and, never knew, really,—not so surely, that New York, if not the country, has something not found here. It makes me feel almost like running back and doing something about it…"[43] His health issues may have shaped the direction of his career, defined the scope of his subjects, and made watercolors preferable to oils or temperas, but they did not make him an artist.

---

[39] Farnham: *His Life, Psychology, and Works. Vol.3*, P.946

[40] Kellner: *Letters*. P3

[41] Farnham: *His Life, Psychology, and Works. Vol.3*. P.994

[42] Farnham: *His Life, Psychology, and Works. Vol.3*. P.940

[43] Kellner: *Letters*, P20

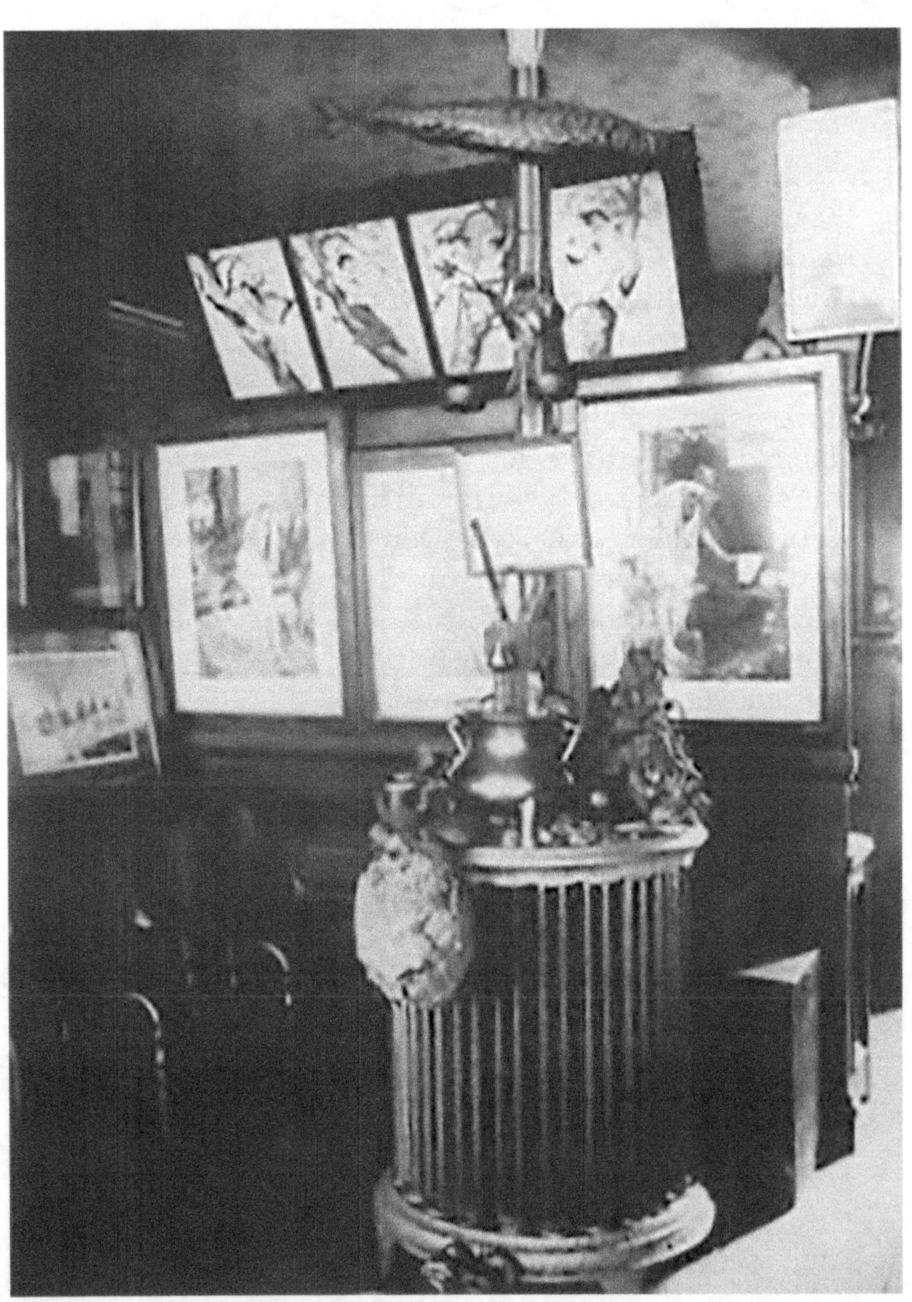

DEMUTH'S DOVE

At Sunnyside Farm in Gap, PA.
Wealth mingled with the Artistic Class.
No common leather book to sign—
Guests etch their names on window glass!
Hardware tycoons and businessmen
May have had a little thrill
From using a glass cutter's tool
Like old John Hancock's Quill.
But such a common workman's tool
Wouldn't suit dear Charlie Demuth.
A grander gesture was required
From an Artist at his zenith.
From his long and slender hand
He removed a diamond ring.
And working, slowly at first,
He made the glass pane sing.
Beneath his name and hallowed date
A Dove of Peace appeared:
Within its beak, a blooming Rose—
A symbol to be revered.
The Guests have all long since gone away
To their eternal rest.
The Heirs have sold the family farm—
But they made a small bequest.
The mural from the cocktail room
And the signed windowpane
They gave to the Demuth Museum
Their glory to sustain.

A GREAT TIME

In his eulogy, a friend said:
"Charles had a great time being himself".
What he did not say—
What he could not say—
Was that Charles
Was rarely allowed
To be himself.
Society kept pushing him
To be a man
To be normal
To stay in the closet.
They labeled him
An invert
A pervert
Sinister.
They blamed his loving—
If overprotective—
Mother for this flaw.
He wasn't allowed to fall in love
And share that love openly.
It had to remain hidden
In the Lafayette Bath,
Or on "THAT" street,
Or behind the mask of
"He's my Cousin".
It filled him with a well
Of loneliness and longing
That he poured out in paint
For all the world to see—
If they were only willing to look.

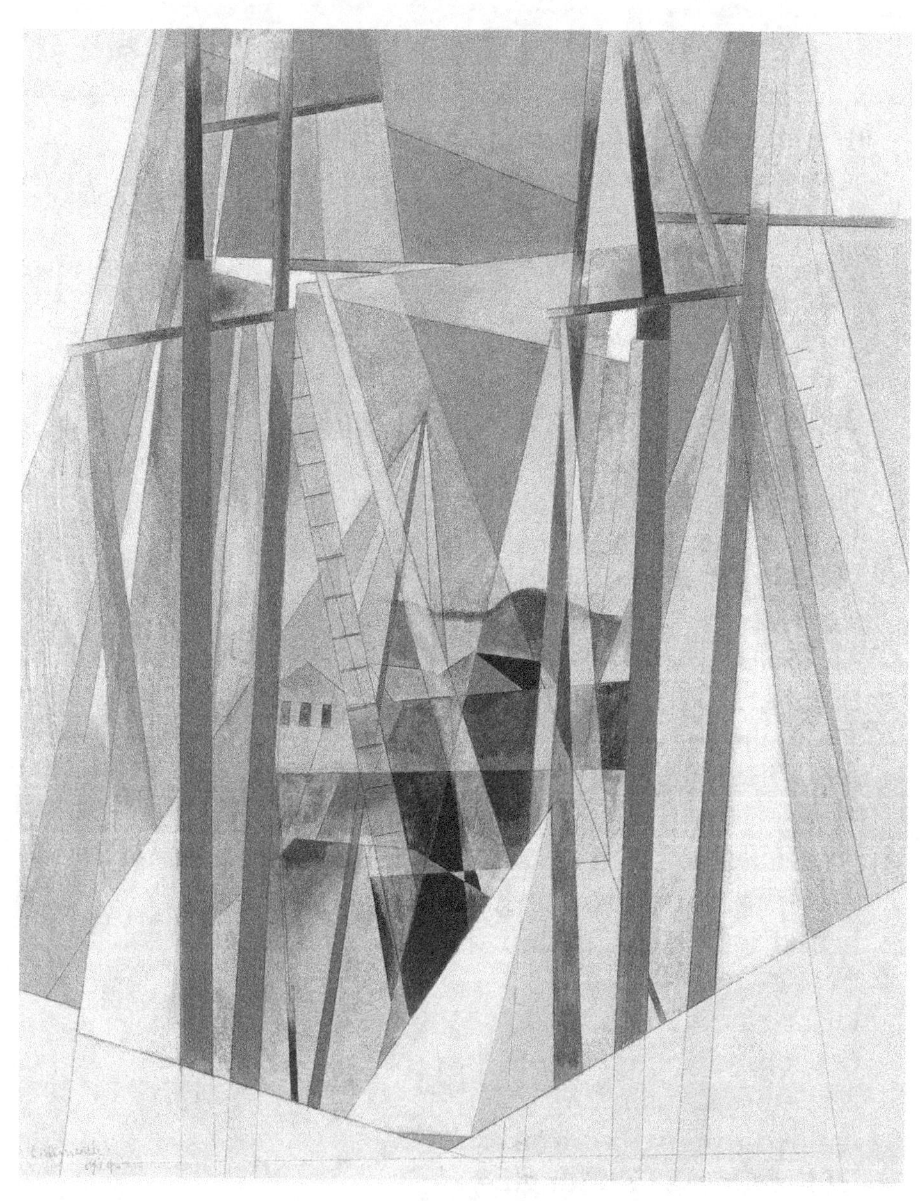

DALI ET DUCHAMP

The first man to compare
The cheeks of a young woman
To a rose
Was obviously a poet.
The first to repeat it
Was probably an idiot.
The ideas of Dada
And Surrealism
Are being repeated
Monotonously.
It is already forgotten that
The Dada leader
Tristan Tzara proclaimed:
"Dada is this!
Dada is that!
Dada is this!
Dada is that!
Dada is nevertheless Shit."
I have been lucky.
I've never had to work for a living.
Also, I haven't known the strain of producing
Or having a pressing need to express myself.
So I consider myself very happy.
I have no regrets.
In the production of any genius
Great painter or great artist
There are really only four or five things
That really count in his life.
The rest is just everyday filler.
I dream of rarity...

I would have wanted to work
But deep down
I'm extremely lazy.
I like living,
Breathing,
Better than working.
When a remarkable person has something to do
Whether it's for his country or not
He can do anything
And it will be extraordinary.

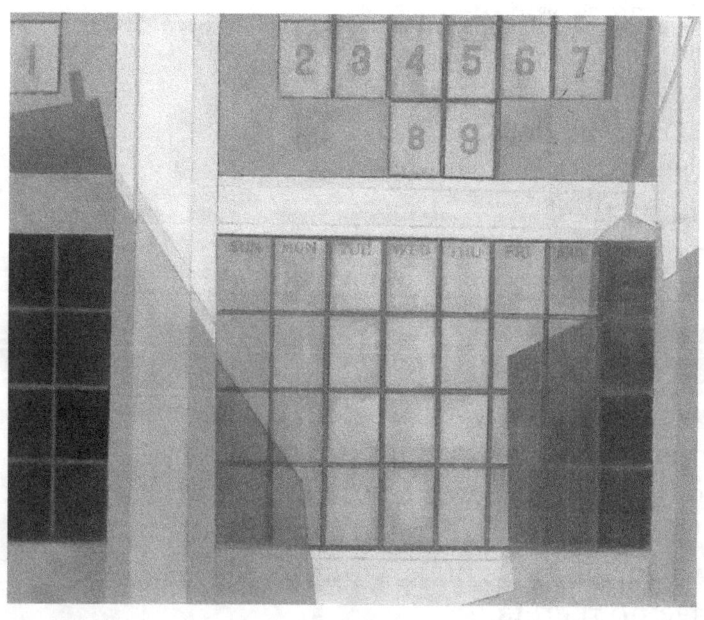

A HIGHER PHILOSOPHY

Ordinary people follow a philosophy
Of Rights and Wrongs,
Of Good versus Evil.
Of Us against Them.
Artists, however, are called
To follow a Higher Philosophy.
Truth is Beauty
And Beauty is Truth—
That higher and more ideal truth
Inherent in the realities of things
And contained by them,
But which are clouded
And hidden in the realm
Of actual life.
Artists must bring out,
Explain,
Make credible and visible
These higher truths
Through the process of his art.
The artist must be afraid of nothing,
Dare to live as one wishes to live,
Have the courage of one's desires,
And seek out every sensation
And manifestation of Life.
Then, Having pulled back the veil
And caught a glimpse of the infinite—
The interconnectedness of all things,
The clouded truths hidden
Behind the ordinary—
The artist must struggle to capture its essence,

To take of it what speaks to his own spirit,
Choosing some details and rejecting others
With the calm artistic control of one
Who is in possession of
The Secret of Beauty.
He must create signposts to the future,
Inspiring people with visions
Of what we, together, can accomplish.
Little else except art is moral.
Life without industry is guilt,
And Industry without art is brutality.
For the words "Good" and "Wicked"
Used to describe the nature of men,
You may almost substitute the words
"Makers" and "Destroyers".
It is by Art that man will be able to
Regenerate his spirit
And build beautiful things
Out of his sufferings,
That he might cry out in triumph
"Yes! This is just where the artistic life
Leads a man,"
Thus shall the World be saved by Beauty.

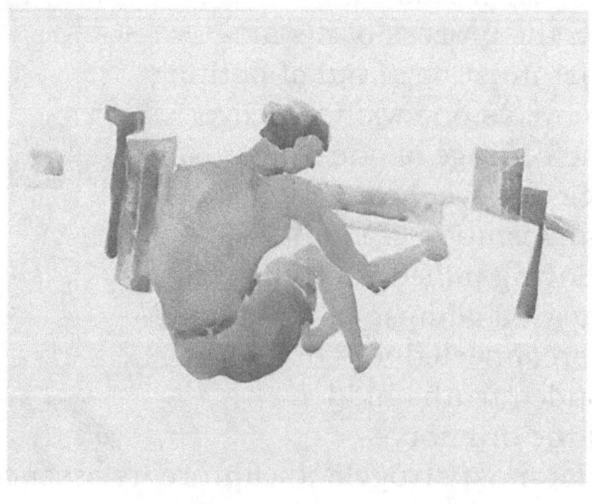

THE QUEERNESS OF CHARLES DEMUTH

During my shifts as a volunteer at the Demuth Museum, visitors are intrigued by and ask questions about two topics more than any others: Demuth's diabetes and his sexuality. Discussions about his diabetes are fairly straightforward and not surprising given the current number of people diagnosed with the disease. The most frequent are: Which type of diabetes did he have? (Type II), How old was he when he was diagnosed? (38 years old), What was the treatment like? (Starvation Diet, later insulin), and did he have any relatives/ancestors diagnosed with the disease? (none that I know of).

Discussions about his sexuality, on the other hand, are more challenging. It has been the position of the Demuth Museum and Foundation that while Charles might have been Gay, there is no proof that he was a homosexual and even if there were, the Museum would not want to "Out" someone who was not "out of the Closet" during their lifetime. They further stress that they want to celebrate his contributions to Art, not his sexuality. They don't want to avoid the topic, but they also don't want to lead with it.

This is a noble aim, and they are not entirely wrong in stating that there is no proof about his sexuality.

I would like to begin by addressing the second point first—That Charles was not "Out" during his lifetime. While it is true that Charles never publicly stated that he was a homosexual (or any other variation in the LGBTQA+ spectrum), we have to remember that to do so in his day would be tantamount to confessing to a crime. Consensual Homosexual relations were illegal in Pennsylvania until 1980, and it wasn't until 2003 that all anti-sodomy laws were declared unconstitutional nationwide.[1] We should also remember that the idea of being "In the Gay Closet" did not exist before the 1960s. "Coming Out of the Closet" does not appear in any known letters or diaries of gay men or in gay literature and stories until then.[2]

Publicly declaring your sexuality was a political act of civil disobedience modeled on the Black Civil Rights movement of the 1950s and 1960s and led to Gay Pride marches as a way of increasing the visibility of this voting constituency.

In fact, the very word "Homosexual" did not exist in the English Language when Charles was born. He lived through a period of rapidly changing attitudes towards homosexuality that has largely been forgotten. The prevailing attitude when Charles was born was that homosexuality was a moral issue. Gay men were referred to as Sodomites, Inverts, Perverts, Degenerates. Beginning in Germany in the late Nineteenth century, there was a shift to a more "scientific" approach that viewed homosexuality as an illness—probably mental—that could be cured with the right treatment. Several unsuccessful attempts at surgical techniques to cure homosexuality were attempted, and many of the psychological techniques continue to this day in "Conversion Therapy". By the end of Charles life, sociologists were expressing concerns about the growth of openly homosexual communities in New York and other metropolitan cities and the effects this "alternative lifestyle" would have in undermining the moral and cultural values of the larger society. The Stonewall Riots in New York galvanized the homosexual community and ushered in the current era of

---

[1] See Supreme Court of Pennsylvania ruling in *Commonwealth v. Bonadio (1980) and* United States Supreme Court, LAWRENCE et al. v. TEXAS (2003), No. 02-102, Argued: March 26, 2003Decided: June 26, 2003

[2] Chauncey, *Gay New York*, p.6-7

openness and political activism, but some of the earlier attitudes continue to persist. The phrase "Coming Out" did exist in the 1910s and 1920s, but it meant something very different. It was modeled on the Debutant Balls where young women would be presented and enter into Society. In the Gay world, it meant joining the larger homosexual community. This often happened at very public events, such as the Transvestite or "Drag" Balls in San Francisco, New Orleans, Baltimore, and New York.[3] We know that Demuth attended at least one of these Balls at the Webster Hall in Greenwich Village with Marcel Duchamp and was a member of the Greenwich Village homosexual community. His self-portrait in the Lafayette Bath House is proof of this. We also know that Demuth wore clothes that fit the coded insignia of homosexuals at the time, such as wearing ties or scarves as belts and wearing "unusual colors".[4] We know that Demuth did this at home in Lancaster, not just in New York, Paris, and Provincetown, Mass.[5] He made no effort to hide who he was, and he was quick to defend anyone's right to individual expression. He is quoted as saying "There is a crusade against Vice in Lancaster. I'm going home to speak for Vice."[6]

It is easy to lose sight of how courageous Charles was by ignoring this side of him.

As to the first point—"Was Charles a homosexual?"—only one person knew for sure, and that was Charles. But as his friend Stuart Davis put it: "If he wasn't, I don't know what he was."[7]

A careful reading of his unpublished manuscripts, letters, paintings, and the stories and interviews given by

---

[3] Chauncey, *Gay New York*, p.7-8

[4] Chauncey, *Gay New York*, p.52-53; Farnham, *Life, Psychology, and Works, Vol. 3* p.991

[5] Lestz, *Charles Demuth and Friends*, p.4

[6] Weinberg, *Speaking for Vice*, p.216-217

[6] Farnham, *Life, Psychology, and Works, Vol. 3* p.971

his friends can, I believe, give us a sense of Charles' romantic desires and relationships.

Before we can begin, though, we need to place ourselves as much as possible within the mindset of Demuth's lifetime. Historian and philosopher Michel Foucault argued that homosexual and heterosexual identities didn't emerge until the 19th century. Prior to that time, the terms described practices and not identity. Foucault cited Karl Westphal's famous 1870 article Contrary Sexual Feeling as the "date of birth" of the categorization of sexual orientation.

As mentioned above, the term "homosexual" did not exist in English during the first decade of Charles' life. It was coined by the Austrian-born Hungarian journalist and human-rights campaigner Karl-Maria Kertbeny in 1868 and first appeared in print in his 1869 German pamphlet "143 des Preussischen Strafgesetzbuchs und seine Aufrechterhaltung als 152 des Entwurfs eines Strafgesetzbuchs für den Norddeutschen Bund" ("Paragraph 143 of the Prussian Penal Code and Its Maintenance as Paragraph 152 of the Draft of a Penal Code for the North German Confederation"). The first known use of homosexual in English is in Charles Gilbert Chaddock's 1892 translation of Richard von Krafft-Ebing's *Psychopathia Sexualis*, a study on sexual practice. The term was popularized by the 1906 Harden-Eulenburg Affair. But even the word homosexual itself had different connotations 100 years ago than today.

In the late nineteenth and early twentieth century, the term "homosexual" only applied to the person in a same sex relationship which adopted the traditionally opposite gender's role; in a relationship between two men, it was the one who adopted the feminine role who would be labeled the "homosexual." Indeed, it would be possible for a man to go through his entire life only engaging in sexual acts with other men and not be considered a homosexual—provided he retained the "masculine" role in the relationships!

Even the term "Gay" had different connotations in Demuth's lifetime. Its original definition of "happy" or "cheerful" began to be used as a code word for locations and events that were tolerant or safe havens for members of the homosexual community. Taverns and cafes in the bowery would guarantee "a Gay Time" in their advertisements to alert homosexual clients they were welcome, and over time the term became associated first with the locations ("Gay Bar") and later with the clientele.

Further clouding the issue is the fact that there were different terms used by those inside and outside the homosexual community, and terms used by both could mean different things. The terms "Faggot", "Fairy", and "Queen" denoted specific types of homosexuals within the community but were used pejoratively (and generically) by those outside the "gay world". For example, the word faggot with regard to homosexuality was used as early as 1914, in Jackson and Hellyer's *A Vocabulary of Criminal Slang*, which listed the following example under the word drag: "All the fagots (sissies) will be dressed in drag at the ball tonight." In the homosexual community, "faggots" were men who maintained an outwardly "normal" masculine appearance, but whose effeminate voice and gestures betrayed their homosexuality; "Fairies" were more androgynous: they would wear a mix of men's clothing and women's make-up; "Queens" would be the only ones who would dress in drag or women's clothing.[8]

We can look at photographs of Charles Demuth and his friends to get a sense of these divisions or classifications, and these might help us understand Demuth's role or orientation within the homosexual communities of Greenwich Village, Provincetown, and Paris. Baron Adolph de Meyer's portraits of Robert E. Locher show him wearing men's suits

---

[8] Chauncey, *Gay New York*, p.12-17

and make-up, which would mark him as a "fairy" in the community, Man Ray's portrait of "Rrose Sélavy" would label his friend Marcel Duchamp a "queen"(at least on occasion), while Arnold Rönnebeck's portraits of Demuth show him using the gestures associated with a "flaming faggot", but none of the more effeminate make-up or clothing to mark him as a "fairy" or "queen".

At this point, it might be useful to answer some basic questions: 1) Was Demuth sexually active, 2) Was Demuth attracted to other men, women, or both, and 3) What did Demuth say/write/paint about romantic relationships?

The answer to the first question is yes. As proof, I offer the story William Carlos Williams told in his autobiography about the night in 1916 when he was urgently called to Demuth's studio apartment on Washington Square:

> *"[W]hen [Dr. Williams] arrived, he found Demuth's back looking 'as though a young tiger had clawed it from top to bottom.' ... They were deep, long digs, recently scabbed over. Charley was worried about infection.*
> *'What in God's name happened to you,' I asked him.*
> *'Do you think it is dangerous?' said he.*
> *'No. But how did you get such digs?'*
> *'A friend."*
> *'Charming gal.'* said I thoughtlessly."[9]

Additional supporting evidence is found in the response Charles gave to the questions "What has been the happiest moment of your life? The unhappiest? (If you care to tell.)" in "Confessions: Replies to a Questionnaire" published in *The Little Review*(New York and Paris), Volume 12, No.2, May, 1929: "Of course, you got away with 'Ulysses' but you couldn't really, with my answers to these two."[10]

---

[9] Farnham, *Behind a Laughing Mask*, p.101

[10] Farnham, *Life, Psychology, and Works, Vol. 3* p.936

To appreciate the implications of this oblique answer, we must remember that when The Little Review serialized James Joyce's "Ulysses" the Post Office seized copies of the magazine and refused to distribute them on the grounds that Ulysses constituted obscene material. In response to John Summer, Secretary of the New York Society for the Suppression of Vice, who initiated the suppression, Jane Heap wrote of James Joyce:

> *Mr. Joyce was not teaching early Egyptian perversions nor inventing new ones. Girls lean back everywhere, showing lace and silk stockings; wear low-cut sleeveless blouses, breathless bathing suits; men think thoughts and have emotions about these things everywhere—seldom as delicately and imaginatively as Mr. Bloom (in the "Nausicaa" episode) —and no one is corrupted.[11]*

The editors of *The Little Review* lost the obscenity trial and were forced to pay a fine of $50.00 each, which nearly led to the closing of the magazine. It makes one wonder exactly how obscene Demuth's happiest moment was!

Answering the second question is a little more challenging to definitively answer. One of the most common questions put to homosexuals is "When did you know?". I am not sure if this is an attempt to learn if people are "born" gay or to find out about a moment of sexual awakening, some experience that first sparks a sense of desire in them. For some, there is a defining moment when they "knew"; for others, it's a slow and sometimes painful process of self-discovery. This process can be further impeded by familial, societal or religious pressures to be "normal".

Charles spent the summer of 1905 in New Hope, PA, painting with Clive Weed and Emmasita Register. Charles

---

[11] Henry Louis Gates, "Book Review: To 'Deprave and Corrupt': Girls Lean Back Everywhere", 38 N.Y.L. Sch. L. Rev. 401 (1993); The Nation, v.254, 898 (1992)

and Weed would visit Emmasita's house on the tow-path "at all hours and eat meals on the lawn under the trees with candles and were the scandal of New Hope, of course… Charles told me the tale of the finale to this romance in his inimitable style. It was all by hints and innuendo but I gathered that he had proposed, and Emmasita…had refused him…"[12] In late 1907 or early 1908, Demuth sent his cousin Pauline Cooper a photograph of a young woman seated on the edge of a fountain, with the message "Marco Sullivan as she is. Incidentally, this will serve to announce the fact that we are engaged." Written on the back.[13] Demuth returned home from his 1907 trip to Paris unwed. In 1914, Demuth developed a "queer kind of feeling for Helene Iungerich…a kind of a crush on her" according to Stuart Davis.[14] But even a mild review of Demuth's paintings will reveal a different story. Demuth asserted in his essay 'Across a Greco is Written': "Across the final surface—the touchable bloom, if it were a peach— of any fine painting is written for those who dare to read that which the painter knew, that which he hoped to find out, or that he—whatever!"[15]

So what did Demuth know, or hope to find out, or ? Outside of the work he did as a student, Demuth rarely painted female nudes. In fact, he rarely painted women at all after about 1916. The same cannot be said about the male figure. The Yale University Art Collection, for example, has 4 Demuth paintings of male nude or semi-nude figures, but only one of a female nude.[16] The University also has a

---

[12] Farnham, *Behind a Laughing Mask*, p.128

[13] Farnham, *Behind a Laughing Mask*, p.128

[14] Farnham, *Life, Psychology, and Works, Vol. 3* p.971

[15] Farnham, *Life, Psychology, and Works, Vol. 3* p.937

[16] Accession Number: males:1995.51.26, 1995.51.12, 1980.83.2, 1995.51.4; Female: 1995.51.33

sketch entitled "Costume Drawing: Devil As Lady"; I will let you decide what to make of that.[17]

Several of Demuth's paintings include self-portraits. Among these are The Purple Pup, Hellhole, Turkish Bath, On "That" Street, and Distinguished Air. In these, Demuth surrounds himself with male companions, either fellow artists in the gay community like Marsden Hartley and Marcel Duchamp or sailors who might moonlight as rent-boys.

To answer the question "What did he hope to find out, or...whatever?", we should pay particular attention to Distinguished Air. Central to the painting is a bronze statue based on Brancussi's "Princess X", an abstract sculpture that most people say resembles a phallus. The Demuth self-portrait—the dapper gentleman with the cane at the left of the painting—is attending the art exhibition in the company of a woman, but he shows no interest in her. Nor does he show interest in the phallic sculpture itself. Instead, he appears to be leaning to his right, gazing at the sailor standing next to him. Or perhaps more specifically, trying to catch a glimpse of the sailor's well-defined buttocks. This suggests the possibility that Demuth was a "top" rather than a "bottom", which is to say he preferred to take on the masculine role in a same sex relationship. If this was true, it is possible by the standards of his day that he did not consider himself to be a "homosexual" at all.

Gertrude Stein wrote in a letter to Ernest Hemmingway: "The act male homosexuals commit is ugly and repugnant and afterwards they are disgusted with themselves. They drink and take drugs to palliate this, but they are disgusted with the act and they are always changing partners and cannot be really happy."[18] We cannot be sure if she intended the remark to include Demuth, who was a friend of hers, a

---

[17] Accession Number: 1995.51.21

[18] Cooper, *The Sexual Perspective*, p.112

frequent visitor to her salon, and a man fond of drinking. Demuth wrote to Eugene O'Neill in December 1919: "I'll try to have February in New York, for what reason I'm sure I don't know, these days of wood-alcohol! I hope we who love drink, for itself, will some time be together in a fair country full of the 'Triu-bang.'...Perhaps I'll go to England. I must have a drink on some street corner of the world soon,—or bust!"[19]

In his painting "Eight O'clock (Early Morning)", the figure seated on the bed at the left seems full of remorse following the previous night's entertainment, but not on the central figure, which might be a self-portrait. Instead the central figure wears an expression of concern for the distraught partner. There is no sense of shame or reluctance in his paintings "On 'That' Street" or "Turkish Bath with self-portrait"; instead, there is an expression of eager anticipation on self-portrait figures. Whether he considered himself to be a homosexual or not, it appears that Demuth was confident and comfortable with his self-identity.

This confidence did not guarantee happiness, and we can detect a sense of loneliness in Demuth's writing. This loneliness, however, is mitigated by the beauty that surrounds him and gives him solace. For example, in his poem "In the Fields", Demuth writes:

I saw a cloud—
No, but the shadow of a cloud
Pass o'er the waving grain.

I saw a bird
Light on a swaying branch
And heard its call.

---

[19] Kellner, *Letters*, p.9-10

One loud clear note
Unto its mate
Who answered not.

I saw a flower
Of golden hue
And sweet perfume.

I touched the flower.
It fell apart
Gold on the green.

And joy and sorrow
Hand-in-hand, passed
O'er the waving grain.

Passed with flower
The bird's love note
And my exquisite hour. [20]

The last phrase, "my exquisite hour", echoes optimistically Shakespeare's line that "Life's but a walking shadow, A poor player that struts and frets his hour upon the stage, and then is heard no more."[21] William Carlos Williams described this sense of "joy and sorrow hand-in-hand" combined with loneliness and isolation in his description of meeting Demuth for the first time. In 'The Great American Novel," Williams wrote: "That look. It was enough. Youth is so rich. It needs no stage setting. Out went my heart to that face. There was something soft there, a reticence, a welcome, a loneliness that called to me."[22]

[20] Farnham, *Life, Psychology, and Works, Vol. 3* p.924-925

[21] Shakespeare, *Macbeth.* Act 5, Scene 5

[22] Williams, Wiliam Carlos. "The Great American Novel", reprinted in *Imaginations* ed. Webster Schott. New Directions, 1970. P.207

In his short story "The Voyage was Almost Over", written sometime after his diagnosis of diabetes and his shortened trip to Paris in 1921, Demuth writes:

"Why, why was everything wonderfully made, perfectly made, and I given the power, above many, to appreciate this wonder and perfection? And yet denied the one thing which would perfect me, truly? If only a little white hand would beckon from without one of those mysterious shadows—then—well, them, to hell with these borrowed ideas. … And hate against some unknown Thing filled his soul."[23]

Many have speculated about what Demuth meant by "some unknown Thing". Pamela Edwards Allara suggested it was his diabetes; Jonathan Weinberg that it was his homosexuality. [24]

I think it's more likely the lingering shadow of a God he no longer believed in but could not completely abandon. Who else could have given Demuth the power to appreciate this wonder and perfection? And why appreciate the creation if not to acknowledge the creator? To see beauty and perfection all around him and yet feel incomplete and imperfect must have been frustrating to say the least. Demuth concludes the story with the lone man returning to his stateroom and searching his steamer trunk for a white box:

The box contained a book; a rare edition of a modern poet. Opening it to the fly-leaf and reading what was written there caused a faint color to return to his whitened face. He reached toward the dressing-stand, got and lighted a cigarette, threw himself upon the couch, turned the pages of the book until he was almost through them, and then read. [25]

---

[23] Farnham, *Life, Psychology, and Works, Vol. 3* p.927-928

[24] Weinberg, *Speaking for Vice*, p.45-46

[25] Farnham, *Life, Psychology, and Works, Vol. 3* p.928

One wonders if this "rare edition of a modern poet" was William Carlos Williams collection *Spring and All*, published in 1922 and dedicated to Demuth. If it was, it might indicate that Demuth was saved by the friendships he had made. In his cover of the gay Russian singer Vadim Kozin's song "Friendship", Marc Almond sings "our tenderness and friendship/gives us more warmth than love could ever give."[26]

This may be a sentiment shared by Demuth. He may have had many lovers—there is a long list of candidates among his friends—but there is only one documented homosexual relationship in Demuth's writing, to an unknown man referred to as "My Cousin" in letters to Henry McBride from 1925-1927.[27]

All the rest were, and remained throughout Demuth's lifetime, Friends.

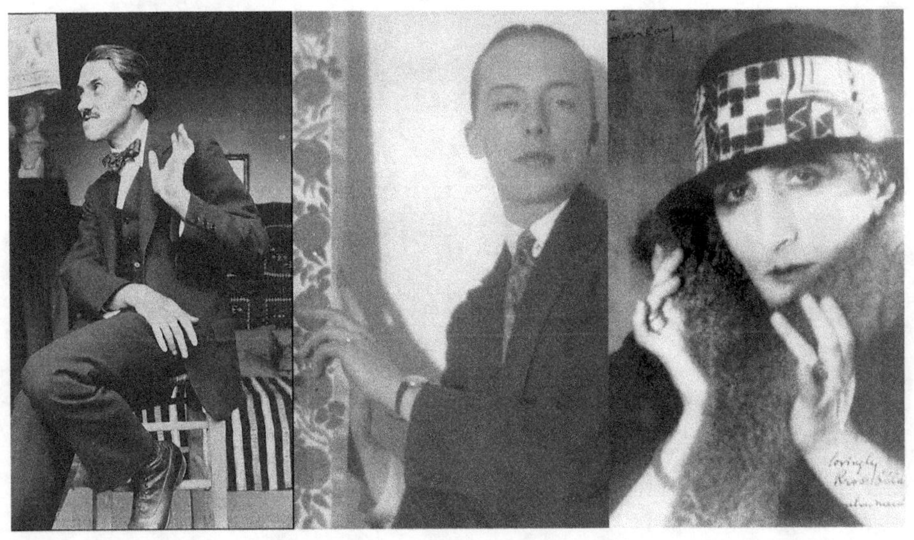

---

[26] Almond, *Orpheus in Exile*, Track 5

[27] Kellner, *Letters*, pp 67-68, 69, 71, 101-102

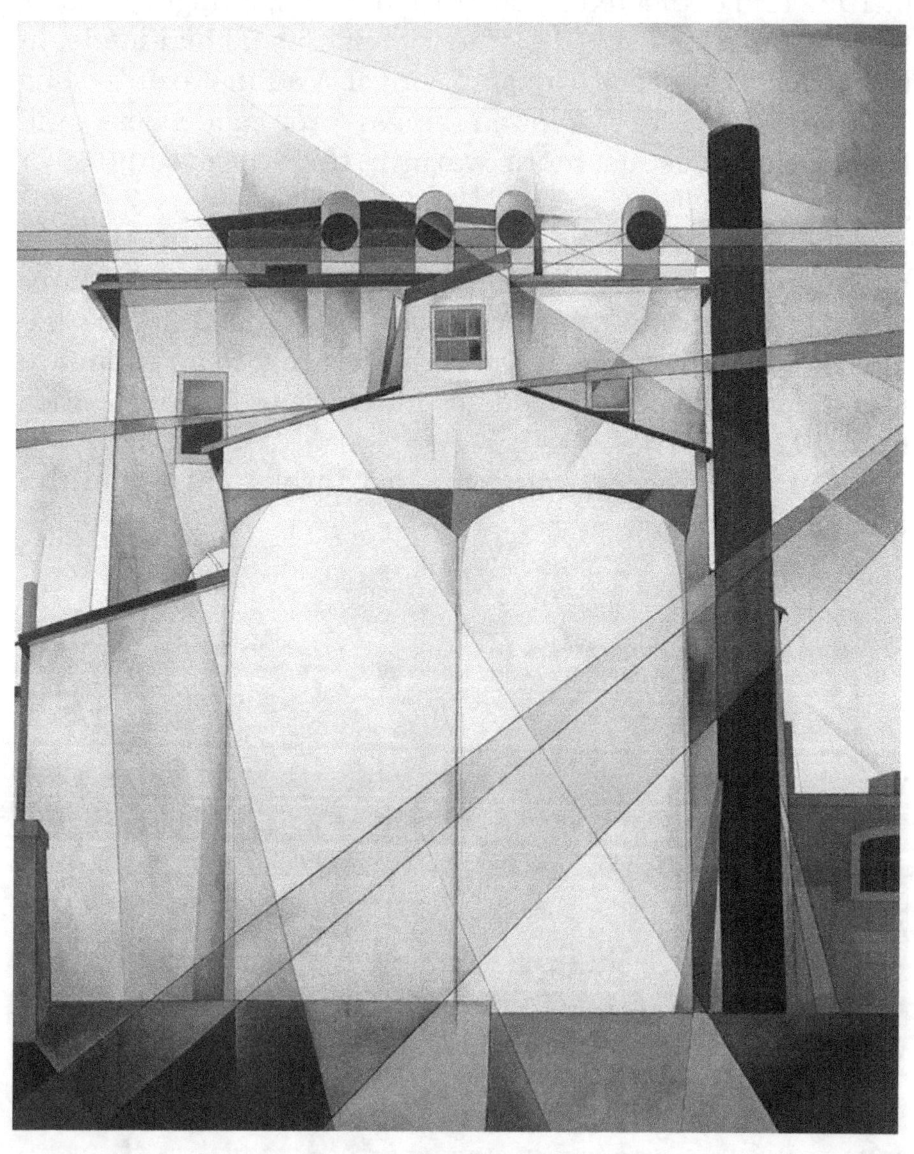

DEMUTH'S "EGYPT"

The description on the Whitney Museum website for Demuth's painting "My Egypt" reads:

My Egypt depicts a steel and concrete grain elevator belonging to John W. Eshelman & Sons in Charles Demuth's hometown of Lancaster, Pennsylvania. Painted from a low vantage point, the structure assumes a monumentality emphasized by the inclusion of the lower rooftops of neighboring buildings (suggesting the more traditional architecture of smaller family farms) at the bottom of the painting. In Demuth's image, the majestic grain elevator rises up as the pinnacle of American achievement—a modern day equivalent to the monuments of ancient Egypt. A series of intersecting diagonal planes add geometric dynamism add a heavenly radiance to the composition, invoking the correlations between industry and religion that were widespread in the 1920s. Nonetheless, Demuth may have intended the title to allude to the slave labor that built the pyramids, intimating the dehumanizing effect of industry on the nation's workers. Moreover, the pyramids and their association with life after death might also have appealed to the ailing artist, who was bedridden with diabetes at the time of the painting's execution.[1]

This summarizes the predominant opinion of Art Historians regarding the inspiration for Demuth's title. I would like to present an alternate interpretation; one I believe would be more relevant to Demuth personally.

---

[1] https://whitney.org/collection/works/635, Copied Sept 10, 2019.

At the start, why Egypt? Demuth had never travelled there and the verdant fields of Lancaster County bare little resemblance to the sandy plains of Giza. The answer, I believe, can be surmised from a comment in a letter Demuth wrote to Gilbert Seldes in November of 1922: "I'm as anxious as the best of "them" towards fame (so called) or publicity."[2]

Shortly after Demuth wrote this letter, Howard Carter announced the discovery of a previously unknown and intact tomb in Egypt's Valley of the Kings and a new wave of Egyptian Revival swept across the world. It would be in keeping with Demuth's desire for "fame (so called)" to tap into the zeitgeist to reach a wider audience through the commentary of the art critics.

The art critics for their part, unaware of Demuth's personal story, saw the looming towers of the Eschelman grain silos as monuments to American Industry on a scale comparable to the Great Pyramids in Egypt. Most likely, Demuth was amused by this assertion, for there is nothing pyramidal in the composition. The cylindrical shape of the grain silos has more in common with the palm-like columns of Egyptian temples than with the polished limestone triangles of Giza. In fact, the Eschelman plant had six silos aligned in three rows of two, although Demuth chose to only show the two at the north end. Collectively, the six would have resembled the columned processional leading into the heart of the temple.

If the silos present the entryway into a modern temple, what idol lies at the heart of it? Past the silos and looming above them in the background is the grain elevator, with the modern machinery to lift tons of grain to the top of the silos. For a man with a hip infirmity, an elevator must have seemed a gift from the gods.

---

[2] Kellner, *Letters*, p.43-44

But why "My" Egypt? Why not "Our" Egypt? So far, this artistic interpretation could apply to any American. What makes this painting personal for Demuth?

To understand the significance, we must first understand the geography of Lancaster, Pennsylvania, Demuth's hometown. The heart of the city is Penn Square at the intersection of King and Queen streets. In the center of the square is the Soldier's and Sailor's monument, erected on the site of the original courthouse and dedicated on July 4th, 1874. This monument acts as the zero stone for Lancaster. From that point, the city extends one mile in each direction along King and Queen street.

Demuth's home at 118 E. King Street was a little over a block from this square. The Eschelman Feed Plant with its massive grain silos was located in the 200 block of North Queen Street, three blocks north of the square and seven blocks south of the city's northern limit. It, like many other factories during Demuth's lifetime, were well within the city limits.

Why does it matter where the grain silos were? Because there is one moment in Egyptian history or mythology that mentions the building of grain silos within the cities. It is the story of Joseph and the interpretation of Pharaoh's dreams in Bible (and Mother Demuth would have made sure that "the Boy", as she referred to Charles, would have known his bible). The story can be found in Genesis chapter 41.

The Chapter begins with Pharaoh's dreams:

"When two full years had passed, Pharaoh had a dream: He was standing by the Nile, ² when out of the river there came up seven cows, sleek and fat, and they grazed among the reeds. ³ After them, seven other cows, ugly and gaunt, came up out of the Nile and stood beside those on the riverbank. ⁴ And the cows that were

ugly and gaunt ate up the seven sleek, fat cows. Then Pharaoh woke up. [5] He fell asleep again and had a second dream: Seven heads of grain, healthy and good, were growing on a single stalk. [6] After them, seven other heads of grain sprouted—thin and scorched by the east wind. [7] The thin heads of grain swallowed up the seven healthy, full heads. Then Pharaoh woke up; it had been a dream."[3]

Pharaoh is deeply troubled by the dreams and sends for his magicians and wise men to interpret it for him, but none are able to do so. It was then that his cup bearer remembered his promise to a fellow prisoner, Joseph, an exile from the land of Canaan.

Joseph is brought from the dungeons, cleaned up, and presented to Pharaoh. Pharaoh tells him his dreams and asks Joseph to interpret them. Joseph responds:

"The dreams of Pharaoh are one and the same. God has revealed to Pharaoh what he is about to do. [26] The seven good cows are seven years, and the seven good heads of grain are seven years; it is one and the same dream. [27] The seven lean, ugly cows that came up afterward are seven years, and so are the seven worthless heads of grain scorched by the east wind: They are seven years of famine.

[28] "It is just as I said to Pharaoh: God has shown Pharaoh what he is about to do. [29] Seven years of great abundance are coming throughout the land of Egypt, [30] but seven years of famine will follow them. Then all the abundance in Egypt will be forgotten, and the famine will ravage the land. [31] The abundance in the land will not be remembered, because the famine that

---

[3] *Genesis 41:1-7, New International Version.*

follows it will be so severe. [32] The reason the dream was given to Pharaoh in two forms is that the matter has been firmly decided by God, and God will do it soon.

[33] "And now let Pharaoh look for a discerning and wise man and put him in charge of the land of Egypt. [34] Let Pharaoh appoint commissioners over the land to take a fifth of the harvest of Egypt during the seven years of abundance. [35] They should collect all the food of these good years that are coming and store up the grain under the authority of Pharaoh, to be kept in the cities for food. [36] This food should be held in reserve for the country, to be used during the seven years of famine that will come upon Egypt, so that the country may not be ruined by the famine."[4]

Pharaoh and his officials like the plan and decide there is no one better suited than Joseph to take charge of Egypt. Under his direction, grain silos are built inside the cities to store the surplus and one-fifth of the harvest from across the country are brought to the cities' granaries. "Joseph stored up huge quantities of grain, like the sand of the sea; it was so much that he stopped keeping records because it was beyond measure."[5]

I am sure the massive silos in the middle of the block on north Queen street, across the street from the old Pennsylvania Railroad station, would have reminded Demuth of this story, especially with the row upon row of rail cars full of grain from around the country glowing "like the sand of the sea" and "beyond measure".

There are further parallels between Joseph and Charles which add resonance to this interpretation. Verse 46 tells us that:" Joseph was thirty years old when he entered the

---

[4] Genesis 41:25-36, New International Version.

[5] Genesis 41:49 New International Version.

service of Pharaoh king of Egypt. And Joseph went out from Pharaoh's presence and traveled throughout Egypt"[6]

Charles turned 30 on November 8, 1913, while he was in Paris, then the Art Capital of the World. He left Paris the following Spring, traveling to New York City and Provincetown, Mass. This was the beginning of his artistic career, a period of abundant creative output that lasted for seven years, until his diagnosis of Diabetes around 1920/1921. Although Charles had never been fat, the 'total dietary regulation in the treatment of diabetes' he received under Dr. Frederick Allens care at the Physiatric Institute left him as ugly and gaunt as Pharaoh's cows.[7] Demuth's friend William Carlos Williams recalled "The result was frightening. Charley faded to mere bones, but was able to live. They occasionally permitted him to be taken home to us for a short visit but I had to return him the same evening. He brought with him a pair of scales and weighed his food carefully. I never saw a thinner active person (this, as I say, was before the discovery of insulin), who could stand on his feet and move about."[8] Demuth wrote to his patron Dr. Albert Barnes in May of 1922: "The treatment has made me very weak,—I do very little."[9] In July, he wrote to Alfred Stieglitz: "Very little left after I do my daily (sometimes, now weekly) painting."[10] Fortunately for Demuth, insulin was discovered around this time, and Dr. Allen administered the first dose in the United Sates in August of 1922. Demuth was reluctant at first to take insulin because of the inconsistent quality of the serum, but in March of 1923 he returned to Morristown after experiencing vision problems and consented to the treatment. Demuth wrote to Barnes:

---

[6] Genesis 41:46 New International Version.

[7] Allen, *Total Dietary Regulation*, 1919

[8] Fahlman, *Chimneys and Towers*, p.74

[9] Fahlman, *Chimneys and Towers*, p.81

[10] Fahlman, *Chimneys and Towers*, p.81

"The serum so far is proving a miracle. It must be magic. I know that I'll wake up and find it only another dream. Have gained ten pounds and can eat bread!"[11] Marianne Moore visited Demuth in Morristown with William Carlos Williams soon after he started the insulin treatments. She wrote to her brother: "We discussed Lancaster, Carlisle, Alice Meynell, Henry James, Gertrude Stein, the flower show, the Williamses plan of going abroad next fall and so on. It was delightful, also heartrending as it doesn't look to me as if Mr. Demuth is going to get well. He is very game, jokes about the cure he is taking and says if you get too much of the serum all you need to do to counteract it is eat a handful of candy; he has diabetes and the proprietor of the sanitarium has discovered a new cure. On leaving he gave me an Easter egg with a rabbit on it from a box of elaborate candy which someone had given him."[12] Writing to Williams nearly 30 years later, she recalled, "I was awed by the fact that he made nothing of his disability and gave the impression of being normal."[13] Despite the success of the treatment, Demuth was still frequently weak and had difficulty finding the energy to work. "I wish that I had some 'go,'—such as yours. Mine seems to be used up these days after two or three hours of work and maybe a walk."[14] 1926 was particularly discouraging for Demuth. He wrote to Stiegliz:"My summer has been a very bad one. No painting,—and such a feeling of it all being too much for the ones really trying. It would be grand to have a bit of background,—the effort to make that new each morning for the day is a great one, too great. Still, if we don't try, will there ever be one?"[15]

---

[11] Fahlman, *Chimneys and Towers*, p.83

[12] Fahlman, *Chimneys and Towers*, p.86

[13] Fahlman, *Chimneys and Towers*, p.86

[14] Fahlman, *Chimneys and Towers*, p.87

[15] Fahlman, *Chimneys and Towers*, p.87

These were not only years of dietary and creative famine for Demuth, but social famine as well. After seven years of living among the greatest living artists and writers in Paris, New York, Berlin, and Provincetown, he was now forced to spend most of his time "In the province". In New York and elsewhere, he was accepted as an equal by artists and writers Demuth both liked and admired. He was given the freedom to be fully and uniquely himself without thought or worry about the reception he would receive from those around him. He was free to pursue romantic adventures free from his mother's ever-present scrutiny. This not only meant a decrease in the inspiration and cross-fertilization he experienced as a member of Alfred Stieglitz's circle, but also a loss of the things which made life worth living for Demuth. To compensate for these losses, Demuth poured himself into his work. "I would love to go somewhere—where I don't know—any place is almost impossible. Maybe it's just something that always goes along with me, that I'm tired of having around, and think a change of place would help me, there. I'm really all right here,—but at times I almost wish I could 'go in for' hysterics; but all I can go in for is another picture. Well, there's almost four new ones to date."[16] If we accept this interpretation, then Lancaster, PA becomes for Charles what Egypt was for the ancient Hebrews: a place of both refuge and oppression. A refuge in that it provided the carefully regulated food he needed to live (courtesy of his mother's devoted care), a respite from the energy-draining demands and distractions of New York's social calendar (a requirement for an introvert, as Demuth has been frequently said to be), and a source of abundance during famine (in the additional income provided by the family's tobacco business and the income provided by renting the ground floor front rooms of his home

---

[16] Fahlman, *Chimneys and Towers*, p.88

as office space); Oppressive as the place of all-work-and-no-play (where he would closet himself in his studio like a monk and paint[17]); of conservative religious values that sought to "suppress and prevent commercialized vice and to promote the highest standard of public and private morals"[18], and where he was forever treated as "the boy".

At first glance, this might appear to be a bleak interpretation. But within the context of Pharaoh's dream, Demuth had cause to be optimistic. The Seven years of famine were coming to a close. If we mark the seven feast years as 1914, 1915, 1916, 1917, 1918, 1919, and 1920, ending with the diagnosis of Diabetes in February-March 1921, the years of famine would be 1921, 1922, 1923, 1924, 1925, 1926, and 1927. "My Egypt" was completed in 1927, along with his homage, "Calla Lillies (Bert Savoy)". The following year, he completed arguably his most famous painting: "! Saw the Figure 5 in Gold". Demuth had passed through the valley of the shadow of death and was climbing up to the pinnacle of his artistic achievement. In 1929, Demuth would write to Stieglitz: "I know, from the quiet of the country, that I won't do many like that one...It's been a long time since I painted a water-colour just that good,—maybe I never did, in some ways,—that I don't much care, unless I get a good price if I sell it, or not."[19]

---

[17] Farnham, *Life, Psychology & Works Vol. 3, p.981*

[18] Twobly, Clifford G. *A Report on Vice Conditions in the City of Lancaster, PA.* American Vigilance Association: Lancaster, PA. 1913. P.5

[19] Fahlman, *Chimneys and Towers*, p.91

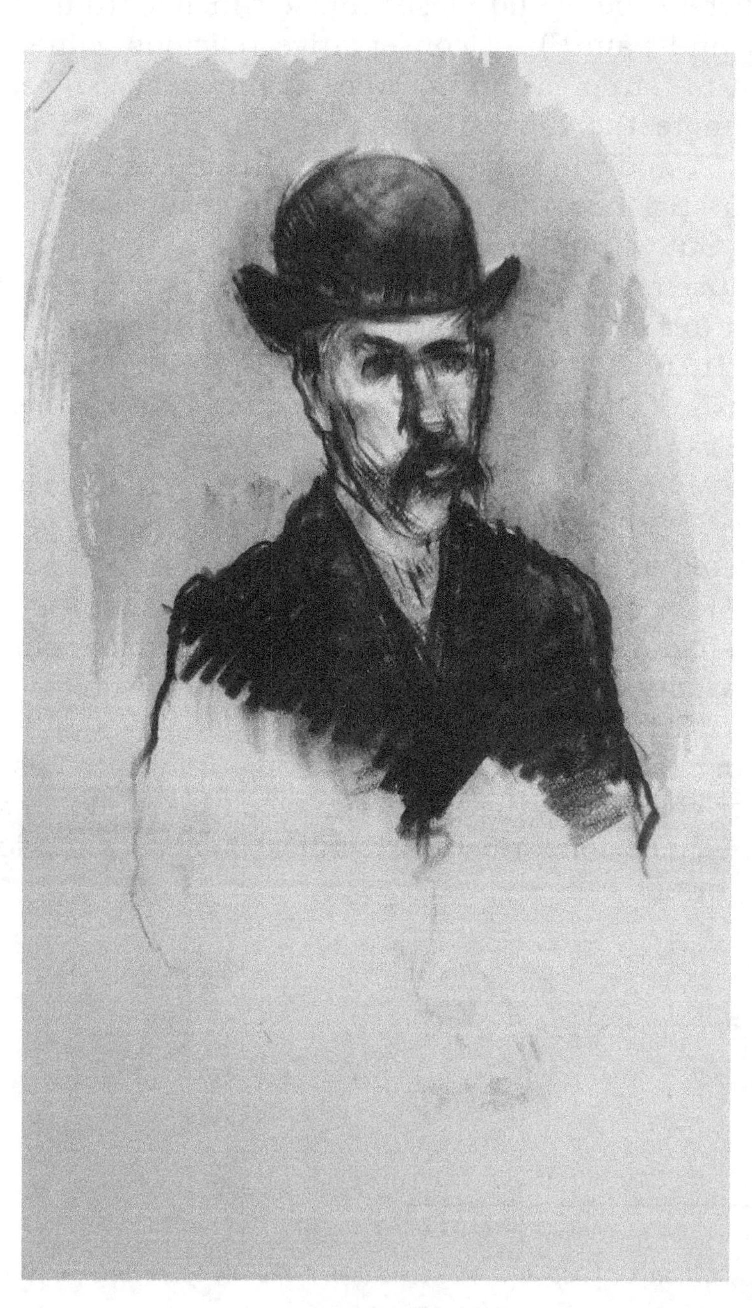

AFTERWORD

People often ask me how I became interested in Charles Demuth. The full answer is complicated and long-winded, involving a friend of a friend who couldn't afford to go to college, 35 Doctoral dissertations, the 10,000 Hour principle, my lack of fluency in Russian and French, and a trip to the Barnes Foundation with my Mom. The short answer is that my life lacked focus, and Demuth's straightforward yet enigmatic life coupled with his assertion that "everything the artist knew, or wanted to know, or whatever" are contained within their paintings gave me something to focus on.

This book is one of the results of that focus. While I have been researching Demuth's life for nearly four years now, this book is not scholastic or biographical in the traditional sense. Instead, it follows in the footsteps for Demuth's friend George Cram "Jig" Cook, who wrote: "I do not aspire to be, in the great sense of the word, a scholar. I hope to prove some day, writing and teaching, a person of tastes and talent, able to help people understand and love rightly the things which are beautiful." I hope this small volume will be considered a work of beauty, in addition to presenting well researched information about Charles Demuth, his circle of friends, and the world he lived in.

Twenty years after Demuth's death, Marcel Duchamp asserted: "Already, Demuth is a legend. Funny how a man can disappear...["1]

In trying to find the man behind the legend, I have had to sort through many apparent contradictions. Many

---

[1] Farnham, *Life, Psychology, and Works, Vol. 3* p.973

friends described him as "Sweet, kind, gentle, and sympathetic," but others insisted he was a "Malicious, narcissistic, arrogant snob." He was said to be shy and retiring, a wallflower—and yet he walked up to a table of strangers in Paris, asked if he could sit at the empty seat at their table, and receiving their consent proceeded to so impress them with his wit that they invited him to have lunch with them every day (and several became life-long friends of his).

Reading his letters and unpublished manuscripts has given me a sense of his voice pattern and inflection, his enthusiastic and passionate stream-of-consciousness style, full of asides and self-deprecations. Looking at his paintings, his letters, and photographs have given me clues to the patterns and colors he loved the most. Demuth is a fascinating mix of hyperbole and understatement. He would compliment friends by telling them their hat or bracelet was "The last word" in that sort of thing. Paintings, to Demuth, were "The final, the Nth whoopie of sight." Charles Daniel, Demuth's New York art dealer, insisted "He wore the most beautiful neckties in New York," but looking at photographs they hardly stand out. Henry McBride described Demuth's bedroom overlooking his mother's garden as "chastely decorated... in white wallpaper with small gold dots at regular intervals." In short, he liked things that were both "unusual and conservative," and above all "elegant."

Reading the various descriptions of Demuth's life by friends and his own hand has often led me to picture those scenes in my mind. Sometimes, the scenes are so vivid that I have been inspired to try to capture them in verse. William Carlos William's descriptions of meeting Demuth in "The Great American Novel" and of their walks in his autobiography led me compose the poem "Carlos." I say compose, rather than write, because I have incorporated Williams (and Demuth's) prose in my verse. In a description of the Marshall Hotel and restaurant—one of Demuth's favorite haunts in New York—I came across a reference to the undercover agents Sonnichsen and and Veness and their work for the Committee of Fourteen, which inspired "Concerned Citizens." Seeing a postcard of a Valentine in the Demuth Museum collection made me wonder what Demuth's response to receiving that card would have been; the answer I came up with became "Valentine Conundrum." "A Living Art" was inspired by Demuth's essay "Between Four and Five" and his philosophy of moments. "In Hospital" combines Demuth's description of a young artist in his unpublished short story "In Black and White" with the imagery from Van Gogh's painting "Garden of the Hospital in Arles." "Little Details" was inspired by Helen Henderson's pen portrait of Demuth, Susan Watts Street's description of his glorifying little details, and a passage in Robert Smythe Hichen's novel "The Green Carnation."

I had originally intended to title this collection *A Green Carnation Amid Red Roses*, a nod to Demuth's "unnatural" nature and colorful personality that would surely have stood out against the backdrop of Lancaster's "Plain People". But that didn't really capture the full scope of this book, nor did it summarize the goal of my research. Duchamp's quote does that much better. The full quote reads "Already Demuth is a Legend. Funny how a man can disappear....There is left only the smoke, the souvenir—the essence, I suppose you could call it."[2]

I hope these pieces capture that essence, and help to give people a sense of the man himself.
Demuth wrote: "Europe was always nearer and dearer, but,—well, you know. What could any of us add to Europe? Perhaps I like to suffer. At times I think I do. It may never flower,—This our State,—but if it does I should like to feel

---

[2] Farnham, *Life, Psychology, and Works, Vol. 3* p.973

from some star, or whatever, that my living added a bit,—for in this flower, if it does, I can imagine Rome in its glory looking very mild."[3]

I think Deem would be very happy with the flowering of American Art, and we should all be grateful for the (ever humble) "bit" his living added.

David T. Shoemaker
August 29, 2019

---

[3] Kellner: *Letters of Charles Demuth*. P.109

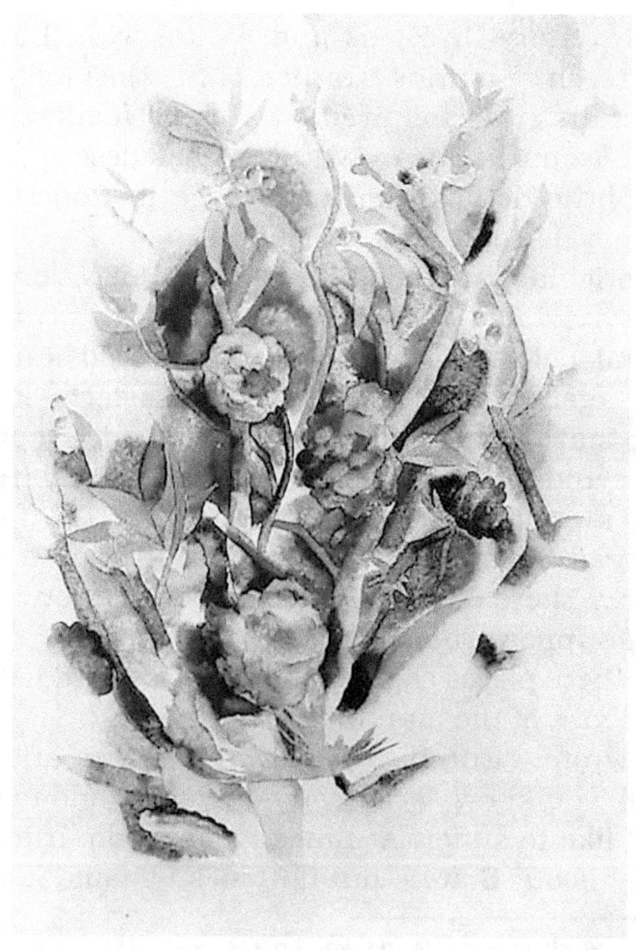

BIBLIOGRAPHY

Allen, Frederick M. and Stillman, Edgar. *Total dietary regulation in the treatment of diabetes*. New York: The Rockefeller Institute for Medical Research. 1919 (reprint)

Beachy, Robert. *Gay Berlin*. New York: Alfred A. Knopf. 2014.

Ben-Zvi, Linda. *Susan Glaspell: Her Life and Times*. New York: Oxford University Press. 2005

Black, Stephen A. *Eugene O'Neill: Beyond Mourning and Tragedy*. New Haven and London: Yale University Press. 1999

Brubaker, Jack. *Remembering Lancaster County*. Charleston, SC: History Press. 2010

Cabonne, Pierre (translated from the French by Ron Padgett). *Dialogues with Marcel Duchamp*. London: Da Capo Press. 1971

Caffin, Caroline. *Vaudeville, The Book*. New York: Mitchell Kennerley. 1914

Cameron, Deborah and Kulick, Don, ed. *The Language and Sexuality Reader*. London and New York: Routledge, Taylor and Francis Group. 2006

Chauncey, George. *Gay New York*. New York: Basic Books (a member of the Perseus Books Group). 1994

Cooper, Emmanuel. *The Sexual Perspective*. London and New York: Routledge and Kegan Paul. 1986.

Eiseman, Alvord L. *A Study in the Development of an Artist: Charles Demuth*. Ann Arbor, MI: ProQuest (formerly Xerox University Microfilms). 1976

Eiseman, Alvord L. *Charles Demuth*. New York: Watson Guptill Publishing. 1986

Fahlman, Betsy. *Chimneys and Towers*. Fort Worth, TX: Amon Carter Museum; distributed by The University of Pennsylvania Press: Philadelphia. 2007

Farnham, Emily. *Charles Demuth: Behind a Laughing Mask*. Norman, OK: The University of Oklahoma Press. 1971

Farnham, Emily. *Charles Demuth: His Life, Psychology, and Works*. Ann Arbor, MI: University Microfilms International. 1959

Fronc, Jennifer. *New York Undercover*. Chicago, IL: The University of Chicago Press. 2009

Gallup, Donald, ed. *The Flowers of Friendship: Letters written to Gertrude Stein*. New York: Alfred A Knopf (A Borzoi Book). 1953

Hapgood, Hutchins. *A Victorian in the Modern World*. New York: Harcourt, Brace and Company. 1939

Hartley, Marsden. *Adventures in the Arts*. Charleston, SC: BiblioBazaar. 2007 (reprint)

Haskell, Barbara. *Charles Demuth*. New York: The Whitney Museum of American Art in association with Harry N. Abrams, Inc., Publishers. 1987

Herrick, Jim. *Unwrapping Historic Downtown Lancaster*. Morrisville,NC: LuLu Press. 2013

Kellner, Bruce. *Letters of Charles Demuth*. Philadelphia: Temple University Press. 2000

Kreymborg, Alfred, et al. *The New Caravan*. New York: W. W. Norton and Company. 1936

Lestz, Gerald S. *Charles Demuth and Friends*. Lancaster, PA: John Baer Sons. 2003

Loose, John Ward Willson. *Lancaster County: The Red Rose of Pennsylvania.* Canoga Park, CA: CCA Publications. 1994

McAlmon, Robert. *Being Geniuses Together 1920-1930 (revised with supplementary chapters and an afterword by Kay Boyle).* San Francisco: North Point Press. 1984

McBride, Henry. *The Flow of Art.* New Haven and London: Yale University Press. 1997

Morgan, William. *Diabetes Milletus: Its History, Chemistry, Anatomy, Pathology, Physiology, and Treatment.* London: The Homœpathic Publishing Company. 1877 (reprint)

Nickels, Thom. *Gay and Lesbian Philadelphia.* Charleston, SC*: Arcadian Publishing. 2002*

Oppenheimer, Rebecca Wolff. *Diabetic Cookery: recipes and menus.* New York: E.P. Dutton and Company. 1917 (reprint)

Schulman, Robert. *Romany Marie: The Queen of Greenwich Village.* Louisville, KY: Butler Books. 2006

Smoller, Sanford J. *Adrift Among Geniuses.* University Park and London: The Pennsylvania State University Press. 1975

Stein, Charles W. *American Vaudeville as seen by its contemporaries.* New York: Alfred A. Knopf. 1984

Tattersall, Robert. *Diabetes: The Biography.* Oxford: Oxford University Press. 2009

Watson, Steven and Morris, Catherine J. *An Eye on the Modern Century.* New Haven and London: Yale University Press. 2000

Weinberg, Jonathan. *Ambition and Love in Modern American Art.* New Haven and London: Yale University Press. 2001

Weinberg, Jonathan. *Speaking for Vice.* New Haven and London: Yale University Press. 1993

Williams, William Carlos. *The Autobiography of William Carlos Williams.* New York: New Directions Publishing. 1967

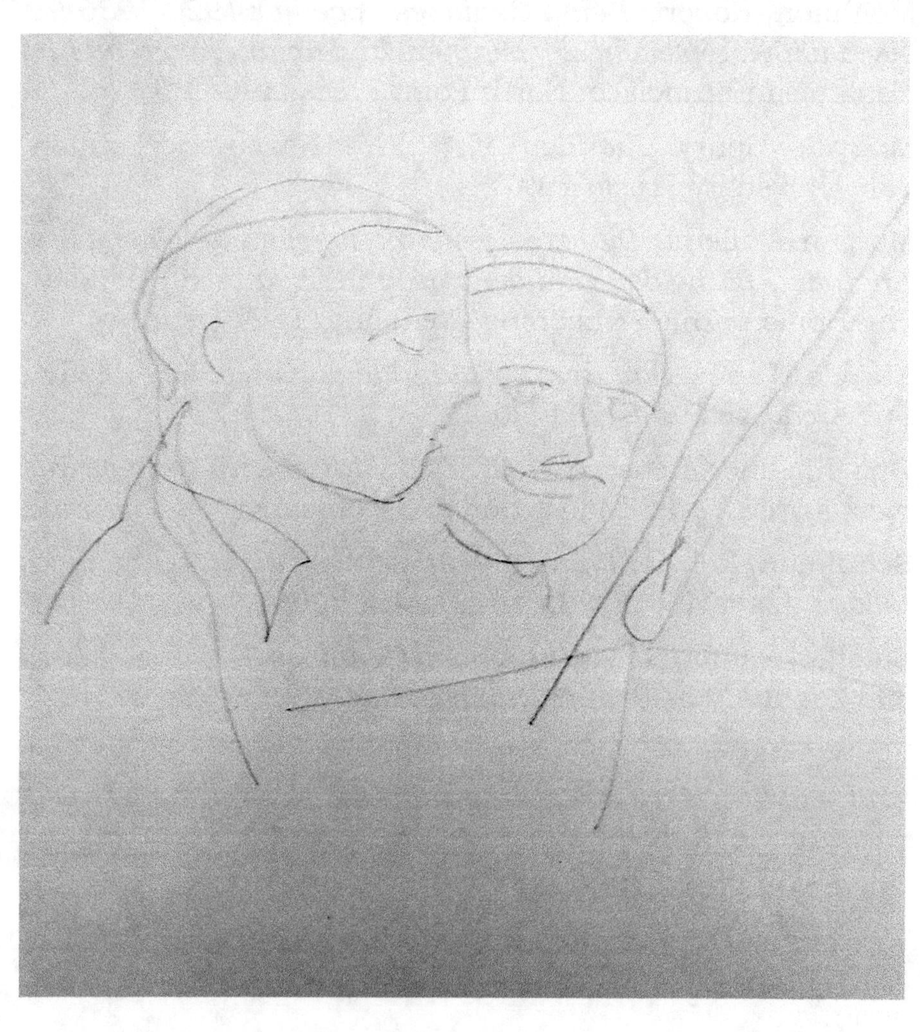

ABOUT THE AUTHOR

David T. Shoemaker describes himself as a Poet, Artist, Philomath, and Endomorph. He was first exposed to the craft of writing poetry in a 5th Grade Poetry Workshop for advanced English students. He has been called an "Historian Poet" for his tendency to weave history, archaeology, and folklore into bardic verse. His poems are included in the "Timeless Voices" (2006) and "Forever Spoken" (2007) anthologies edited by Howard Ely. In 2017, he released the CD "Bardsongs" which featured him reading his poetry.

He is currently working on developing a series of walking tours in Lancaster PA based on the life and works of Charles Demuth, an early 20th century American artist who helped introduce modernist principles to American Art, founded the Precisionist Movement, and influenced such diverse artists as Georgia O'Keeffe, Jasper Johns, Andy Warhol, and Robert Indiana.